Primary School Projects
Planning and Development

Derek Waters
Director of ILEA Primary Management Studies Centre

Heinemann Educational Books
London

Heinemann Educational Books Ltd
22 Bedford Square, London WC1B 3HH
LONDON   EDINBURGH   MELBOURNE   AUCKLAND
HONG KONG   SINGAPORE   KUALA LUMPUR   NEW DELHI
IBADAN   NAIROBI   JOHANNESBURG
EXETER (NH)   KINGSTON   PORT OF SPAIN

British Library C.I.P. Data

Waters, Derek
Primary school projects:
    planning and development.
    1. Elementary schools—Great Britain—
    Administration
    I. Title
    372.1.3'6   LB2901

ISBN 0-435-80916-4

Printed and bound in Great Britain by
Biddles Ltd, Guildford and King's Lynn

Contents

Acknowledgements

As teachers we are influenced in all kinds of way by those with whom we work, and I owe a great debt to those who have helped to shape the way I have worked with children.

There are the children, of course, whose reaction to the various projects always encouraged me to seek out better and more varied ways to approach the work.

The various staff I worked with also showed me that there were different ways of achieving particular results; staff who were prepared to cooperate in joint enterprises; teachers who were prepared to give generously of their time to engage in training programmes in school to sharpen particular skills for the benefit of the children.

I am also grateful to the staff of the Diploma course at London University Institute of Education who for the last ten years have discussed with me the various ingredients of a project.

I would like to thank Sheila Hilder for her typing of the manuscript.

Introduction

During his voyage to Laputa, Gulliver received an invitation to inspect the Academy of Projectors at Lagado. He graciously accepted, announcing (I am) 'a great Admirer of Projects and a Person of much curiosity and easy Belief, for I had myself been a sort of Projector in my younger days'.

I also was a 'projector' in my younger teaching days, particularly during the Spring and Summer terms when, with my final-year class, I could turn my back on the period of 11-plus iniquities and a syllabus delineated by traditional academic disciplines. For several weeks at a time we experienced the wholeness of knowledge by working together and building up a store of information about some theme which interested us. In the late 1950s and the 1960s there was a general relaxation of academic rigour in primary schools as authority after authority did away with its examination-bound selection procedures.

I had some six years of working through a project approach when I was appointed to the headship of a new primary school. This was an exciting period because I was able to work alongside teachers who were equally enthusiastic about the project approach. I noticed that as confidence grew, members of staff regularly combined with colleagues teaching similar age groups to develop a project of mutual interest. In this way they were able to make full use of each other's different talents, skills, interests and inclinations. Once a term at this particular school we selected a theme and, for three or four weeks, classes worked on various facets of it. At the end we had a considerable project to which each age group had contributed and of which each child felt a part.

Some fifteen years ago I became involved in teachers' workshops where once or twice a term a central theme was explored over a weekend by fifty enthusiastic adults. As well as the development of some valuable ideas which could be transferred directly back into their schools, the teachers learned the basic ground rules of project work. More importantly, perhaps, they also learned what it actually feels like to do many of the things associated with project work – to make a model castle or rocket, to set up a science experiment to 'discover' things, to paint a large picture with a dozen other people . . . and perhaps most salutary of all, to try and use a workcard written by someone else. I have also had the good fortune of working on different environmental projects with teachers where, again, success depended on their active involvement. Teachers are sometimes hesitant in workshops because they themselves have not participated in the kinds of activity in which they expect their children readily to engage. But in activities such as those above everyone soon relaxes and joins in.

Although for the teacher, the role of 'projector' is a demanding one, most teachers are capable of providing the necessary effort, imagination and discipline to make it work. I am reminded of the lines which come near the end of Richard Bach's book *Jonathan Livingston Seagull* (Pan Books 1973): 'Look at Fletcher. Lovell. Charles-Roland. Are they special and gifted and divine? No more than you are, no more than I am. The only difference, the only one, is that they have begun to understand what they really are and have begun to practise it'. I hope that primary teachers will work on projects with their children, because in helping pupils to learn how to learn they will themselves begin to understand 'what they really are'.

Derek Waters

1 Projects in the Primary Curriculum

Primary school project work probably represents the two extremes of the enviable and the awful.

In the best examples one can observe young children confident and hardworking, learning from their teacher, their friends and other resources both inside and outside the school. There is an atmosphere of real educational purpose in such classrooms which are, by turn, workshops, studies, seminar areas, briefing rooms and exhibition places. Personal and group experiences are at the centre of the varied activities as the project develops shape and direction, finally reaching a climax of collective achievement.

At its worst, the project is identified with inept teaching lacking both planning and purpose and carried out in a classroom environment notable for its chaos and noise. In such places one can observe a tragic waste of talent, opportunity, time and materials. Although frequently defended as being 'child-centred' and 'activity-based', such examples proved easy meat for the knives of the Black Paper writers and other detractors.

Somewhere between these extremes, projects continue to be carried out in almost every primary classroom in the country. In most classes this activity will take up between fifteen and twenty per cent of the available time. It is important, therefore, to use this time profitably. We need to consider carefully what we are trying to achieve and whether, by adopting a project approach, we are working in the most efficient way.

In search of a definition

The interchangeability of terms used by primary teachers when speaking about projects confirms that there is no generally shared understanding of what constitutes work of this nature. Teachers speak of topic work, thematic studies, environmental activities, local investigations and integrated studies as well as project work. Each term has a different shade of meaning for the individual teacher and school. It follows that pupils too must have an interesting view of what constitutes project work and it is certainly not always clear to them what the teacher expects them to do.

I would prefer to define a project in the following terms. A project is a complete piece of work in which the children have made individual and group contributions towards the whole. Information and impressions are gathered, organized, recorded and communicated through a variety of media. First-hand experience, gained through investigation and problem-solving, is particularly important. For each project a number of goals, some broad and others quite specific, will be determined by the teacher.

The Plowden Committee in their Report 'Children and their primary schools' (HMSO 1967) referred to the value of adopting such an approach 'to make good use of the interest and curiosity of children, to minimize the notion of subject matter being rigidly compartmentalized, and to allow the teacher to adopt a consultative, guiding, stimulating role rather than a purely didactic one'.

Reading the instructions

Too often in education, teachers are encouraged to embark upon a particular methodology without fully understanding the basic principles which underpin it and the merits and demerits of working in that particular way.

For instance, Harold Rosen in *The Language of Primary School Children* (Penguin 1973) suggested that 'the whole of our educational system is peopled by busy copyists . . .' with 'vast quantities of useless information about uninteresting subjects all industriously copied from secondhand sources'. More recently, the Bullock Report (HMSO 1975) reiterated this complaint by stating that much of the written work associated with topic work amounts to 'no more than copying'.

Generally headteachers approve of the project approach but do not offer guidelines on how such work should proceed. Because no clear aims and objectives are laid down by the school, few attempts are made to evaluate the product with any kind of objectivity.

In their report on Primary Education in England (DES 1978) HMIs were rather muted about project work. They voiced their concern about the 'random and superficial' nature of some geography and history work and said, 'The elements of these subjects were frequently taught as topics or projects which sometimes resulted in repetitive work rather than an extension of children's skills and knowledge.'

Where the teacher abdicates responsibility and allows each child to choose its own topic, a very limited range of titles is proposed. 'Fashion' and 'Football' are the predominant selections of girls and boys respectively, perhaps occasioned by the availability of illustrations to cut out and arrange in a scrap book. What is worse, the whole procedure may be repeated year after year if the do-it-yourself principle is allied to a laissez-faire attitude on the part of the teacher.

Over-enthusiastic teachers may also be guilty of a number of faults. They may be 'leave-no-stone-unturned' fanatics who are determined to drop in a contribution from every subject discipline in the mistaken belief that in this way every need will be catered for in a balanced project. Similarly the 'famous-person-slept-here' zealots can find all kinds of unlikely starting points in their neighbourhood to allow them by a series of tenuous links to circle the world.

These pitfalls can, however, be avoided by the careful planning of a project, clear aims and objectives, and decisions on how best the children might proceed in their studies.

It is important that the whole staff should meet to discuss principles and practice and come to conclusions on a number of key issues; for example, should history, geography and science be taught as separate subjects or should an integrated approach be adopted? If the latter is decided on, how can each teacher ensure that the right balance is achieved? If project work is seen as the right vehicle for primary school work in the humanities and sciences, could an agreed programme of work be established which would avoid repetition of subject matter and still allow for some individual choice. Could it also allow for the inclusion of some important and interesting topical event? Where a more traditional treatment of subjects is adopted selection of units of work is inevitable. It should also be recognized that it is impossible in project work to give universal coverage to all knowledge appropriate to primary children (even if there could be any agreement on what this is). A selection of suitable topics agreed by the staff should ensure that every child is introduced to a wide range of issues. The formation of a school programme is examined in detail in Chapter Two.

When project work is discussed by a group of teachers some agreement should be sought on how much time can be given over to it. As a result of the recent scrutiny of primary school practice and concerns about the basic skills, there is a danger that the curriculum could be so narrowed that little would be available other than language and mathematical teaching. In *The School Curriculum* (DES 1981) this point is dealt with emphatically. 'There is no evidence that a narrow curriculum, concentrating only on the basic skills, enables children to do better in these skills; HM Inspectors' survey suggests that competence in reading, writing and mathematics may be improved where pupils are involved in a wider programme of work and if their skills in language and mathematics are applied in a variety of contexts.'

Three hours a week would seem to be an acceptable allocation of time for project work. Where much of the class creative work in music, art, craft and language work is related closely to the centre of interest, then four-and-a-half hours could be added to encompass these activities. Some schools prefer to block in periods of their timetables each week to ensure a careful monitoring of work. Other schools prefer to be more flexible in their approach so that it is relatively simple to increase the amount of project time during particular weeks. This would be an advantage when excursions are planned, together with their associated preparation and follow-up work, or the climax of the study is being reached. Adjustment can be made in other weeks so that a balance is achieved.

For the youngest children, a short project of a few days is all that can be expected while lower juniors can sustain interest for four or five weeks. Upper juniors could be presented with a topic lasting half a term, and in some cases a whole term could be allocated for a particularly absorbing project. Teachers should be ready to provide breaks between work of this kind. The intervening periods can be used to develop understanding of the world in which they live, concepts of history, some introduction to work in elementary science, and an appreciation of religious beliefs and practices – that is to say, fundamental concepts which have not featured in any of the year's project work.

In addition to the firm proposal that teachers should consult each other when making decisions about the choice of projects, it is necessary to make the same point where team-teaching is the pattern. Within each team, the leader will confer with his or her colleagues. The various strengths of the teachers should make for greater richness because of the diversity of interests and experience which is available to a larger group of children. However, it is important that the team leaders should confer to provide a good balance of project activity which will take account of what has gone before and what is to follow.

In some schools where the building is a conventional one and where teachers are accustomed to working independently, opportunities could occur for parallel classes to share a project. Once again, the shared expertise of two or even three teachers working cooperatively should benefit the enlarged group of children. To take this idea one stage further, schools may decide to select one large project in which each class and every teacher can be involved. For such ventures to be successful, consultative meetings should take place under the guidance of a strong chairperson (and not necessarily the headteacher). Particular aspects of the super-project can be selected bearing in mind the age and interests of the children and the wishes of members of staff. The generous sharing of resources, ideas and specialist teaching skills would all contribute to the success of the enterprise. Six weeks would be the maximum time for this type of activity – more probably it would be run for a month, with the very youngest children sharing many of the experiences of the whole project but only being actively engaged for a week as the climax approaches.

Catering for individual needs
Increasing numbers of primary schools are now obliged to introduce vertical grouping when allocating children to their teaching groups. In such circumstances it is particularly important to increase the number of options of projects to ensure that no child needs repeat a particular

study. Careful record-keeping and regular discussions should eliminate this possibility.

The professional task of the teacher is to identify and accommodate individual needs. The children within a class manifest a great diversity of abilities, interests and backgrounds of a social and cultural nature. The demands upon the teacher to meet the requirements of this complex situation are great. In vertically grouped classes we introduce yet other variations – those of age and maturity. Within the class the teacher must attempt to meet individual needs. The survey *Primary Education in England* (DES 1978) reported that 'Where work was not matched to the children's capabilities, it was insufficiently demanding . . . in the case of the more able, the work was considerably less well matched than for the average and less able.' Work must be available which is both stimulating and challenging to every child. To organize this will be seen to be more essential in a vertically grouped class since there is likely to be a wide range of abilities present.

In addition to individual activity, some work will be more suited to a small group. This can be as small as a pair – a group size not often suggested as an option except in physical education. Personal choice can enter into such pairings but sometimes the perceptive teacher will create coalitions where talents are complementary, or where one child may lead another successfully. Where larger groups are involved in project work five or six children can work well together provided that they are presented with a venture which will respond to group activity. Creative work is often the most successful of these, especially where the composition of the team offers various talents including leadership.

In a well planned project with outside experiences, teachers should provide opportunities for personal work and group activity. In addition they should include class lessons, demonstrations and discussions. Each situation will be determined by the particular objectives which the teachers wish to achieve, as well as bringing necessary variety to the work – another advantage of the project approach.

The aims and objectives of a project

The curriculum of a school could be said to be all that is planned on behalf of the children. The setting of aims and objectives provides a reason for the exercise and a purpose for the planning. These early considerations enable the teacher to establish both the content of a programme and its direction. Once the work gets under way, some modifications will be made as teacher, pupils and task interact.

A single objective may be reached by one or more activities; one single educational experience can result in the achievement of many objectives. The project approach by its very nature can enable a child to reach many goals, some which will be unique to one topic and others which can be achieved by almost every project. It is important for the teacher to appreciate the full potential of working in this way and make explicit what are seen to be the desirable outcomes of such studies.

Factual content

In the past it seemed that the basic reason for studying historical, geographical and scientific subjects in school was to enable the child to acquire facts, and any evaluation was limited to a regurgitation of the same information. Thinking over the last decade or two has brought about a dramatic change in emphasis. The accumulation of data is no longer considered to be the top priority because there are many other more important goals to work towards.

The children will learn about 'space', 'food', 'water' and so on because of their inherent curiosity and response to a stimulating project, and it is important that they should become enthusiastic about the information they are gathering. But more valuable to them will be the ways in which they acquire the data and what they do with it.

There will be a body of knowledge relating to each study which it is important for the children to have. The children need to understand the meanings of the words they read, hear and use, and their vocabularies will be extended during a project as will their knowledge of the world in which they live.

Basic concepts

It is important that children should have a conceptual understanding of the world. The teacher must try to arrange experiences which are appropriate to each child's stage of development. These will be followed by discussion and explanation and, it is hoped, understanding of, for instance, what is a home, a family, a neighbour, a foreign country, a democracy, a faith, etc.

Early work by Hilda Taba (*Curriculum Development, Theory and Practice* 1962) and more recently *History, Geography and Social Science 8–13 Project* (Schools Council 1971) proposed key concepts could be consciously brought out in many project themes. The Taba concepts are: *causality, conflict, cooperation, cultural change, differences, interdependence, modification, power, societal control, tradition* and *values*. The Schools Council project team identified the following as being important: *communication, power, values and beliefs, conflict/consensus, similarities/differences, continuity/change, causes and consequences*.

The Liverpool team working on the Schools Council Project said of their proposals: 'So with the key concepts it is necessary to realize the Project's seven concepts are an arbitrary, though not irresponsible selection. Others might choose differently. For this reason the Project puts forward that teachers should develop their own list of key concepts'. Thus it is important not only to decide upon particular concepts to develop in a project but for each teacher to discuss with his or her colleagues what he or she is attempting to do. This dialogue will be valuable in determining continuity and coherence throughout the school.

Investigation skills

Investigation skills will be developed from direct experience which should be an integral part of every project. Opportunities must be provided for children to observe various phenomena out-of-doors. Such observation work will usually be preceded by the preparation of the class, and a search for evidence. The teacher needs to select the area for fieldwork with care to ensure that it is suitable. It is too risky to assume that things will be there; early reconnoitring will verify whether the particular tree, animal spoor, fossil or type of building material is present. A random search may be appropriate in quite a large area, where the children are older and have some training in systematic field study, but for younger juniors training will be necessary. Accidental discoveries will be made from time to time and these should be accepted and pursued by both children and teachers. Such finds most frequently occur in a seashore or rockpool investigation.

Identification is an important skill and many projects will present opportunities for its development, for example, of birds, plants, motorcars and architectural features. The use of identification keys and books of reference should be introduced to encourage the children to look for important features and learn both popular, local and official names of plants, animals and things they encounter.

Details of many of the observations made should be recorded in some form or other which is appropriate and therefore useful. This activity may be preceded by classification and ordering of observations. In some cases interpretation may take place, and details of this should be written down. On other occasions it may be more convenient and more relevant to carry out the analysis procedures back in the classroom, when patterns and relationships can be more carefully considered by putting a number of pieces of evidence and observation, possibly from different people, alongside one another.

As well as exploratory work out-of-doors, investigation skills can be developed by the setting-up of experiments both inside and outside the school. When a phenomenon has been noted, the child may wonder why it has happened. A tentative explanation might be suggested, and experiments set up to prove or disprove the hypothesis. If the original suggestion or explanation is not confirmed than further work can then take place. The process of problem-solving in this systematic way should help the children to learn techniques to find out what they want to know in similar or different situations.

Study skills

Closely linked with the previous activities will be the equipping of the children with skills enabling them to glean information from a variety of resources. Most information is found in print form but data is increasingly available through other media. School libraries usually stock pictures, maps, charts, kits, slides, and sometimes audio and TV cassettes. Children need to learn how to use libraries and should be introduced systematically to classification systems, catalogues, and ways and means of extracting the information they need from one or more resources. For the most able, techniques of scanning, speed reading, note taking, and comparing information and opinions from a variety of sources should be introduced.

Initially teachers will need to provide close and careful guidance as simple skills are introduced. The ultimate aim should be to help the children move towards independent learning with the enthusiasm and ability to raise their own questions and then to answer them satisfactorily.

Just as record-making during observation activities was stressed, so it is important for children to be able to make adequate notes on their own researches. It cannot be assumed that children will pick up the techniques automatically and presentation skills should therefore be introduced. These should include layout, use of pictures and diagrams, references and so on. Project work can also be presented in a variety of forms, from personal notebooks to group folders and wallchart displays. The overhead transparency, photograph and even film should be available, especially in the upper part of the junior school.

Manipulative skills

Within the project, opportunities will occur for the children to handle a variety of instruments, from tape measures to instamatic cameras, and compasses to portable tape recorders. While some children may have these and other more sophisticated machines at home, some formal training in their use needs to be included within school time to ensure good results. As with investigation and study skills, assessment of progress and the recording of such information should be made for every child.

Creative skills

Where a school integrates many areas of work within the project approach, even if only in a partial way, there will be opportunities for the development of skills which will be seen to have a real purpose. Just as the basic skills of reading, writing, speaking, listening and number work are used directly within a topic, so activities relating to music, drama, movement, art, craft and creative writing are naturally introduced because they illustrate and enhance aspects of the study.

Project work stimulates awareness and aesthetic appreciation of the world around us. Within the creative subjects, children will have a chance to express themselves and in so doing learn various skills in a stimulating way. Once again careful record-keeping should ensure that the next teacher will be able to build upon earlier work carried out and experiences gained.

Communication skills

In each of the skill sections above, some element of communication has arisen. The act of recording is a most important technique to develop and this is associated with the business of publication. Children need to learn how to present in written and pictorial form the results of their researches, fieldwork and analysis. The various methods of providing graphical representation of a survey – making a map or a three-dimensional model of a castle or a Viking warrior, reproducing the profile of a pond – should be introduced. Such items will probably appear at an exhibition and what the children say, and how they say it, are considerations which the class and the teacher should keep in mind.

On their fieldwork visits, when receiving a visitor in their classroom, or during normal class activities, conversation will be going on. There are many aspects of formal conversation, for example, interviewing, which the teacher can help his or her children with.

Other modes of communication may form an integral part of a project – for example, lecturettes, a talk to accompany a set of slides or a playlet acted out during Assembly. These again are areas where attention can be focused on skills. Children should be encouraged to be spontaneous and lively in their written and speech forms, but unless their work can be read, heard and understood, then no communication has taken place.

Teachers must discuss both written and oral work with children in such a way that they are encouraged and stimulated to do better. Neatness, spelling, accuracy and diction are important virtues. We fail children if we don't promote these in project and other school activities.

Personal and social development

Since the use of the project method in many cases assumes an integrated approach to learning, it will come as little surprise to discover that the goals decided upon will come close to being a set of universal aims for primary education. Since we are concerned with the whole child, societal and individual aims will be present throughout a study, particularly since many of these goals cannot be realized by any other means.

Within a well-planned project it should be possible for a child to learn to be self-reliant, show initiative, develop a sense of responsibility, to persevere, to accept advice and instruction and develop confidence in his or her own ability. Each child should be willing and able to act as a leader, and at other times to respond to others' leadership demands. The child should be aware of the differences between people, and be ready to accept their unique qualities, performance, cultural differences and religious sensitivities. Each child should learn to cooperate with others and share materials, ideas and skills. As well as personal behavioural development, the teacher will want to ensure that certain other changes take place. These will include the development of positive attitudes towards work, property, the environment, injustice, etc.

The various objectives outlined in this chapter have significance beyond the immediate demands of a primary school projects. The skills, knowledge and attitudes acquired as well as their own personal and social development should help the child to face both the secondary phase of education and adult life with confidence.

2 The Anatomy of a Project

Having adopted a physiological term for the title of this chapter, it seems appropriate to describe the basic framework in Fig. 1 as the skeleton of the project.

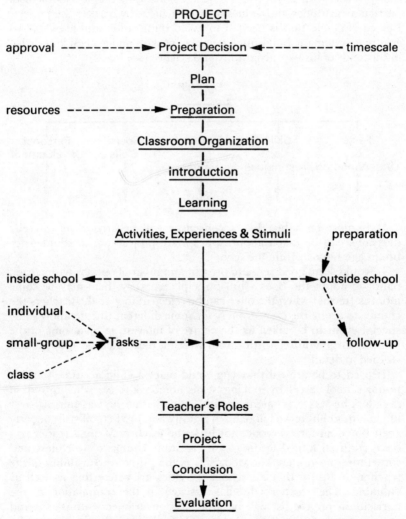

Figure 1 The skeleton of the project

In this chapter these aspects of the project will be discussed.

Choosing the Project

A large proportion of the aims and objectives listed on page 5, especially those linked with cognitive and social skills, and the development of particular attitudes and values, can be achieved whatever the project. But careful selection is needed to avoid duplication and above all to ensure a systematic build-up of a variety of skills and general knowledge in the fields of history, geography and science (see Fig. 2).

Figure 2

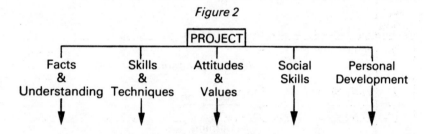

It is most probable that a consensus will be arrived at whereby decisions can be taken about appropriate projects to be adopted for broad age-bands within the school.

It would seem good sense to present a number of options within each band; to adopt the Book Club principle whereby there may be some months (terms) when the offer can be rejected; to give the teachers the chance to argue the case strongly for some different title; to allow some special event to be taken as the centre of interest; to give some of the projects large umbrella titles from which a part could be adopted and studied in detail.

It used to be argued that you could place a child accurately in his junior school career by looking at his notebook to see which group of invaders he was campaigning with, and whether he was musing over life in a mud hut or an igloo. Such rigidity and predictability frequently spelt boredom for everyone, not least the teacher. Many a reader will have endured forced feeding of indigestible chunks of worthless and sometimes out-of-date knowledge. It is the prime responsibility of the teacher to ensure that all school activities are interesting as well as valuable. The teacher who has assisted in the compilation of the curriculum project list will be in a position to inject enthusiasm and imagination into the chosen topics. This will be further heightened by the shared development and collection of resource material related to each project. There is still flexibility in the system as described above to allow for personal and school initiatives, the grasping of opportunities which a school centenary, some new exploration of space, or a dynamic TV series offers, because within all of these many of the same selected objectives will apply. The fact that 'water' has not been studied would be passed on to the next teacher, who could then put it back into the programme. Many primary schools operate a flexible timetable and additional time can be 'won' to include a short study on some topical matter, without abandoning the agreed programme.

Teachers will readily recognize many old friends in the matrix of projects in Figure 3.

Figure 3 Project themes

Age group				
6+	Animals	Homes Prehistoric Animals	Our Street	Christmas
7+	Early Man	Farming	Shops	The Sea
8+	Explorers	People Who Serve Us Our Town	Water	Romans
9+	Food	Weather Normans	Communications Air	Space
10+	Europe	Elizabethans Victorians	Transport Local Study	Our Bodies

It can be fairly argued of course that Animals could be very satisfactorily studied by third-year juniors, and that infants will enjoy Space as a topic, while the oldest juniors may get a great deal more out of the study of the Romans if they were to leave it until the final year rather than look rather superficially at the topic in the second year. But whatever the decision, a staff discussion would perhaps produce some useful suggestions to rationalize an obviously unsatisfactory situation.

Criteria for Choice

In making a choice of subject either for such a school programme or on an individual basis, there are some factors which are helpful to keep in mind:

1   The project should be of interest to the children. The teacher's skill and ability to motivate the children has an important bearing on this factor. One of the teacher's main functions should be to enlarge the interests of children and to extend their horizons.

2   The project should be of interest to the teacher. While it will not ensure success, the teacher's enthusiasm about a particular theme is likely to communicate itself to the children, as is a lack of keenness. Since there is a period of preparation, the teacher may already have reached and passed the peak of enthusiasm by the time the children are beginning their work. However, the children's response, perhaps guiding the project in a particular direction, will sustain the teacher.

3   The project theme should take account of the age, aptitude, ability and experience of the children – and any other differences which might exist, e.g. maturity, social background, culture and race. The teacher has a unique knowledge of the background and capacity of the children, and will know therefore whether the subject matter or the method by which it is going to be approached will be appropriate. One must be wary of pitching one's expectations at too low a point. Consider, too, Bruner's controversial statement: 'The fundamentals of any subject can be taught in some intellectually honest fashion to any child at any stage of development.' Even if we find that that statement, presented in such a dramatic fashion, unacceptable, we can agree that primary children are now learning all kinds of things which would have been thought impossible a decade ago. We also need to take account of the developmental levels proposed by Piaget and others. Older children are better able to cope with more abstract ideas, more academic approaches and logical discussion than are younger children. But the boundaries dividing these different levels should be flexible.

4   The project can be linked in some way with a study which has gone before and one which might follow it. Continuity and progression should aid understanding. Good record-keeping and consultation would increase the chances of this happening.

5   The project should involve the learning of new skills, ideas and facts. Quite often this consideration does not arise when the teacher chooses the project, or while it is in progress.

6   The project should embody useful things to know and to do.

7   The project should enable the child to learn at first hand, rather than rely upon reference books and other aids exclusively.

8   The project will therefore enable the class to experience stimuli outside the classroom and school. The time of the year may be a significant factor in the choice of topic. Harsh weather conditions may inhibit learning opportunities, or indeed the chance to observe living organisms.

9   An integrated approach to a project will be more in line with the way in which children view their world.

10   The teacher would ensure there are adequate resource materials available to provide both information and inspiration for a particular project.

11   The project 'area' needs to be sufficiently large to enable an abundance of activities and experiences to be planned for individuals, small groups and the whole class. Too many so-called class projects fail because there is insufficient opportunity for everyone to be involved, or not a wide enough variety of tasks for children to engage in.

12   The project should take account of the child. We need to remember that by and large a child is curious, active, adaptable, interested in living things, influenced by his peers, likes to belong to a group and has a passion for collecting.

13   There should be at least some flexibility in the project to allow for children's enthusiasms. By making the project as open-ended as possible, the teacher's and the children's differing perceptions can complement each other.

14   Infants and younger juniors are not mature enough to deal with concepts of historical time or sophisticated social studies. So in considering the appropriateness of a project for a particular age-group the following schema should be kept in mind:

5 years ⟶	13 years
Here and near	Distant
Familiar	Unfamiliar
Immediate	Past/Present/Future
Simple	Complex
Concrete	Abstract

15   The children must be actively involved in the project both inside and outside the school. If the teacher is simply teaching a lesson out-of-doors, the result will be little different from the situation where the children are sitting passively in their desks.

Of course it is possible to ignore many of these criteria and still have a successful project, but for those teachers developing their skills in this area it may be helpful to consider each aspect.

So if we return to the question of selection and consider the choices which are available a number of categories can be decided upon, and from these a selection can be made. For instance a project could be about 'Me'; for an older child the choice could be about groups of which the child is a member – the family, the street and near neighbours, the school and friends, the village/town/suburb/city; we can now move from 'Us' to 'Them' and focus the study on other groups of which the child is not a member – people in other environments, in this country, in the UK, in Europe, other parts of the world; the dimension of time can also be included and the children can study their own people and others in earlier times. Nor must we forget the important imaginary world around which a project can be developed.

Some teachers may prefer to study the school surroundings, and proceed under various headings, e.g. People, Places and Things; What's here? What was here? What will be here? and try to help the children make sense of their immediate environment. Some might argue that this could be too restrictive in some environments.

Yet another series of headings can be drawn from basic human activities – playing, learning, working, growing up, being in a family, reproducing, growing old, moving about, communicating, making, growing, buying, selling.

Abraham Maslow is an American behavioural scientist who has introduced a theory based on human needs. He postulates that man, being a creature of needs, must satisfy his requirements and desires at one level, before he seeks to respond to those drives of 'higher' importance. The main headings are:

Self-Actualization
Self-Esteem
Social Needs
Safety Needs
Physiological Needs

Each of these headings can provide us with appropriate, relevant and interesting project areas:

1   The self-actualization needs include: mastery of self and situation, and realization of full potential.
2   The self-esteem or ego needs include: responsibility, praise, recognition, achievement, self-respect, knowledge.
3   The social needs include: love, companionship, importance of belonging to a group, identification.
4   The safety needs include: health, security, protection, law and order.
5   The physiological needs include: water, food, air, sleep, shelter, warmth, survival, sex.

If the school aims include helping children to understand themselves, to take account of others, and to make some sense of the world as it was, is and might become – and indeed help it to become – then human needs would suggest a variety of possible projects. Already in this section the areas of food, water, air and shelter (homes) have been suggested. Under the safety needs, topics such as the police officer, castles, weapons, the rescue services, the United Nations, will provide insights into this particular area. The reader might like to look at all the levels of need and devise a list of projects commonly met with in the primary school and possibly a few new ones. 'Achievement' – under self-actualization – suggests a number of different studies, from explorers and adventurers who explored the lands and oceans of the world, and beyond into space, to those who invented the great machines, the wonder drugs and so on.

Yet another 'programme' was devised by a group of teachers on an in-service training course, which was looking at content as well as skills and attitudes.

1 How we dress, shelter, feed, keep warm, keep well, keep safe, communicate.
2 Food, production and processing, natural wealth, manufacture, trade, transport, energy and power.
3 Groups we belong to – family, school, town, nation. Countries which are important in the world today.
4 Exploration, discovery, learning.
5 Independence, interdependence, cooperation – people, nations, aid.
6 The Earth, humans, animals, plants. Agriculture. Fishing. Conservation. Seasonal changes. Life cycles.
7 Culture, tradition, values. Religion and faith.
8 Art. Music. Drama. Leisure.

It seems appropriate to consider how these things apply elsewhere in the world, and how they have evolved through time.

The BBC – with Schools TV and radio broadcasts – and Independent Television, produce programmes usually of high quality and interest. Details of the titles and content for each programme and extensive teaching notes are available to teachers before term begins. Many series run in two-year cycles but can also be recorded on audio or video tape for later use, without contravening copyright regulations.

In selecting a project the teacher needs to be aware of any particular bias, and if a historical project dominates the autumn term, and a geographical one the spring term, a scientific project in the final term would achieve a balanced programme. If the teacher is unable to achieve such a balance it will be important for the head to try to ensure that those children do come under the influence of a teacher who has more scientific leanings at some time in their primary school life.

In a team-teaching situation, this anomaly is unlikely to arise to such an extent as each member of the teaching group may offer different expertise, talent and knowledge. Hopefully the head considered this when developing the team. Since a large number of children as well as teachers are involved in a cooperative teaching project, the choice of topic should allow for a greater variety of activities and experiences. Each term a different teacher in the team can select a topic and do the major part of the preparation and provide the necessary leadership and direction.

In some cases a whole school may adopt a project and, as in the team-teaching situation, there must be sufficient scope to permit a variety of tasks at different age-levels. One usually successful primary project is The Four Elements, with perhaps the first-year children taking Air as their centre of interest, the second year Water, the nine- and ten-year-olds Fire, and the oldest children studying Earth.

The staff may decide to study the local environment, and each teacher, when discussing the proposal, will adopt a suitable aspect to work through with the class.

'Europe' makes an interesting school theme with each class adopting a different country. 'Beginnings' is another title which allows for a wide range of choice – anything from the Beginning of the Earth to the Beginning of Space Travel. In each case the results of the project can be brought together into an interesting and often spectacular display.

It will be the responsibility of the head or senior teacher to enthuse the staff, and obviously the idea of a whole-school project should not be overworked. Perhaps once a year would be sufficient, and the project might only run for a few weeks. Certainly it would be difficult for infants to sustain their interest for longer than that.

Obviously a teacher or indeed the school cannot cover everything. Decisions will have to be made about what projects will be attempted. There will be gaps, just as there are in most schemes of work, and these will need to be included in a discussion of continuity between primary and secondary schools. In this way duplication could be avoided, and agreement reached on areas which each school could cover.

The selection of a project can very much involve the children. For instance, the teacher can discuss with the class what they might like to do as a project during the following term. By carefully considering their particular enthusiasms, the teacher can adopt an umbrella title which would encompass all or most of the suggestions. On the other hand the broad title can be given, and then a preliminary discussion takes place on particular aspects which would engage the interest of individuals.

No lesson is as effective as one which grows out of a natural situation. If this can be linked with some first-hand experience and practical activities, then the initial impetus will be maintained. Of course one assumes that the teachers' response to the situation and subsequent interest will match that of the children. The duration of such a project may depend upon interest, the available resources and other required support. But in adopting a multi-disciplined and multi-directional approach and travelling into unknown territory, the teacher will have to be very confident.

In the case of individual projects, the same applies, because the teacher still retains the responsibility to make sure that the child is learning and developing at a satisfactory pace. Once again this policy demands a great deal of experience on the part of the teacher who needs to be able to manage time well and knows where and how to give attention to each child. What must be avoided is a situation in which a solitary child works in isolation on a personal project, and has no audience for the final production. A successful personal project involves the teacher in persuading the child to move outwards and forwards, thus gaining a variety of experiences to enable him to learn more about himself and the world he is growing up in.

Planning and Preparation

The necessity for the twin activities of *planning* and *preparation* seems so self-evident that it should hardly require mention. Yet they are often inadequately 'done or even so neglected that we need to remind ourselves of their importance and form.

Planning and preparation need to be done in plenty of time. In other words, with the type of project which is the subject of this book, pre-planning should begin months rather than weeks before the opening activities. This timespan allows for the fact that other work in class is still going on (probably on the current project amongst other educational activities), teachers have additional responsibilities in school, and lead private lives as well.

Once it has been decided what the project is to be about, it is useful to start a notebook in which to compile the plan. Busy teachers have not always sufficient time to research every project in detail and it is helpful to see how others have tackled a particular subject, so it is useful if school project details are filed. They will provide at the very least a pool of initial ideas which can be adopted, adapted or rejected. The second part of this book is based on the premise that project plans, and other educational ideas, are for sharing.

The 'quest' can begin with a series of basic questions which will help the teacher formulate ideas:

What are we going to do? (not a cry of despair but rather an effort to make sure we have made a firm decision about the project title).
Can we justify the choice of this project?
What particular aspects will the children be interested in?
What do we want the children to find out?
What are the different facets of the project?
Can all or some of these facets be put into a sequential order?
Will it be possible to provide experiences and activities which will adequately match all the abilities of the children – particularly the least able and the gifted?
What are the fundamental features of the project which it will be important for everyone to know? to understand? to be able to do?

What are the features of the project which are less essential, and so could constitute various options within the project? (thus ensuring that as much of the project is covered as possible).

How can we achieve the results we are seeking? (The choice of method(s) will depend upon a variety of dependent and unrelated factors – the teacher, the individual children, the project, the school norms, the parents', governors' and LEA's expectations, and so on.)

What do we need to ensure success? (resources, support, aid, new skills, a work plan, ideas, time).

How do I arrange to obtain or develop these resources? (It may be necessary to compromise on some if not all items. It may be important to gain the head's approval for the plan if the activity moves away from the normal school activities or requires additional support.)

What activities and experiences will we want to include in the project to ensure that the general aims as well as specific objectives we have set, will be reached?

Flow-diagrams

A flow-diagram is a useful device to collect together early random ideas on aspects of the project which might be included in the study. It may be necessary from time to time to begin again, having re-grouped some of the first thoughts on the theme. By associative thinking, the learning web begins to take a shape which can become: a basis for particular emphasis, for complete coverage, for optional choices; a record of the development of the project (by ticking off items accomplished); a guide for the remainder of the project, and a plan which the children and teacher can use.

The teacher can seek ideas from colleagues and from children while the project is in progress, as well as during the planning stage, and add these to the diagram.

The traditional approach is to consider the project through conventional subject areas. The way in which some if not all ideas emerge and are seen to spread equally across several boundaries will reinforce the principle of integration which is a feature of the project method (Fig. 4, p. 21). Linked with this approach is one which considers the work from the point of view of the activities which the children will engage in. After these headings have been decided upon, some specific ideas could be developed (Fig. 5, p. 21). Alternatively that type of framework can be dispensed with and the web used to gather together in a random way all aspects of the project for possible inclusion (Fig. 6, p. 22).

It perhaps needs to be repeated that we are at the planning stage. Things never quite go as intended in the classroom, especially if the teacher is taking account of the needs, understanding and interests of

Figure 4 The multi-discipline project

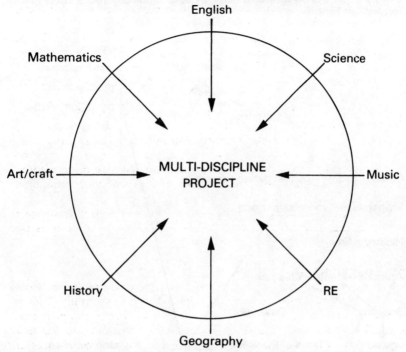

Figure 5 The activity-based project

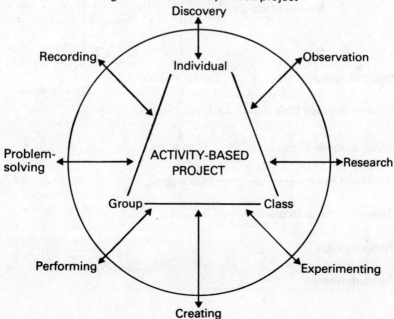

Figure 6 The project web – linking by association different aspects of a project on Time

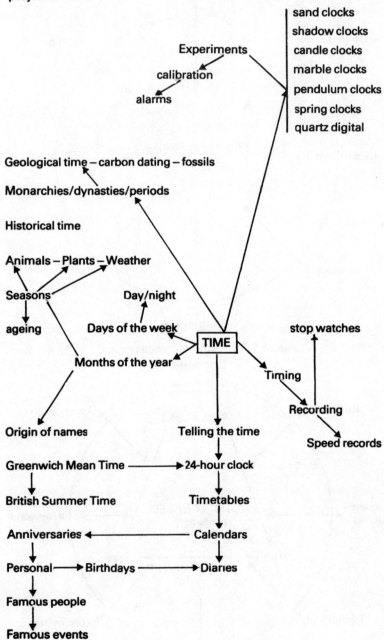

the pupils. New opportunities will occur during the project which should be seized and incorporated. But this in no way invalidates preliminary planning by the teacher. By considering the plan, and the amount of time available, the teacher can decide what constraints will have to be applied, what deadlines set, as well as the special key events which will be featured in the project. These will include bringing in special resources, e.g. films, speakers, materials, using broadcast material, arranging for outside visits, and the culmination of the project. The events may be thought of as a linear progression, and the resulting plan used as a diary, appointment and activities register (Fig. 7, pp. 24–5). The horizontal divisions can be increased to include other groups of people who may be involved at any stage. In the example provided the teacher would decide whether some different items needed to be included or excluded, but the basic matrix can be used for any type of project, with a shorter or longer timescale.

Classroom Organization

Adequate preparation of a project is vital. The same kind of attention to detail is required in the day-to-day organization within the class. In the project method where a child is not doing work identical to that of his or her neighbour, and where a variety of resources including the teacher are being used, there will be movement and discussion. All activity needs to be purposeful otherwise the children themselves will adopt a casual attitude about the whole process, and see 'project' periods as being less important than other school work where greater restrictions are placed upon them. In most respects the same standards need to apply in, for example, the children's presentation of work, the amount of effort they are putting into the various activities, their determination to complete an assignment. The teacher needs to make this plain to the children – both when the project is introduced, at regular intervals, or when there has been some mishap, misdemeanour or slackness.

Instructions must always be clear. The children need to know what they are allowed to get for themselves, where they can get it, what they must do with resources when they have finished with them, what they should do with completed work, what they should go onto next, those people they can seek help from – including peers, how they should store incomplete work safely until the next time they are able to carry on with it, etc.

For the class to carry out their work effectively it will be necessary for children to move about at various times, work in different areas of the classroom, operate in groups, function in large spaces, have access to large surfaces, use apparatus which requires mains electricity supply,

Figure 7   A linear plan for a project on Fire

PROJECT COUNT-DOWN	− 3 MONTHS	− 2 MONTHS	− 1 MONTH	− 1 WEEK	WEEK 1
TEACHER	Project decision Reading	Develop learning web Plan scope and sequence	Resources gathered Develop work-cards Plan excursions	Letters to parents introducing new topic Details for children Friday	Introduction Lead lesson Workcard procedure Details of resources
CHILDREN			Completion of last project Final display	Asked to think about project – consider aspects of particular interest	Series I Workcards Work in pairs Art as main creative activit
SCHOOL	Head authorizes resources Check previous projects		Secretary duplicates materials Ancillary covers workcards		Head requeste to take 'Fire' as assembly theme
LEA		Request loan resources books	Approves excursions	Project box arrives	Films delivere
PARENTS			Check those who have useful experience		
OTHERS			Arrange visits Arrange local library contacts		

WEEK 2	WEEK 3	WEEK 4	WEEK 5	WEEK 6
Film on volcanoes Check workcard responses with children Preliminary visit to museum	Film on *Fuels and Energy*	Film on fire-fighting Act as adviser for personal projects Preliminary visit to firestation		Plan display with team leaders Check all work folders Evaluate project Invite D/Head to comment on project
Class follow-up to film – discussion, frieze, plan assembly Series I Workcards	Series 2 Workcards Work options Visit to museum	Assembly on 'Fire' Series 2 Workcards Group activity	Visit to local firestation Personal assignments	Personal assignments Prepare class and corridor display Prepare quiz team to answer questions on 'Protect Yourself From Fire'
Music teacher assists with songs linked with theme	Drama specialist assists with play on 'Fire'	Visit of Fireservice to school with engine	Letter to parents, VIPs – invitation	Class visits to Fire Exhibition View film
			Loan of display materials from Insurance Company and Fire Service	
Parent who has experienced a fire describes what happened	Grandparent describes the 'blitz'			Visit exhibition Answer quiz Ask questions of young experts Fire Officer opens exhibition

engage in activities which of necessity need to be near a water supply, or use a projector or TV monitor which require a dark corner of the room. Because of the nature of some of these alternatives, as well as their variety, it is important that the teacher reorganizes the available space to meet the requirements as far as possible.

This may involve some movement of furniture – which can be carried out with the aid of a small group of children – labelling of special areas and instructions to be followed. It may be necessary to allocate space and materials on a rota basis if the class is a large one and/or certain activities are likely to be very popular.

Where such arrangements are temporary they can be detailed on the blackboard; more permanent allocation of time and space may have to be written up on a chart. If such a chart is compiled each week it can ensure a fair system for all the children and prevent too narrow a range of activities for certain children who, if unchecked, might spend the whole of half a term painting quite happily, or on an exclusive diet of writing.

In a school where team-teaching is a feature, or where there is part-time teaching help available, or an ancillary worker or parent volunteer, the use of this specialized adult help needs to be planned for. Where the teacher knows the strengths and interests of the additional helpers, maximum benefit can be gained from such forward planning.

Arrangements need to be made for the classroom information resources to be stored efficiently, and invitingly; for writing materials and art and craft items to be placed neatly in accessible places; for space to be allocated for the science apparatus, for three-dimensional models, fabric work, etc. – which may or may not be completed – so that the classroom does not take on the appearance of a second-hand shop and rupture relationships with the caretaker. As school rolls fall, so more space becomes available, and while not suggesting the empty room next door should become a dump, it is useful to store the large model of a farm in there neatly on tables, or pin the almost-completed frieze of Invasion Overlord onto a vacant wall. An under-used cloak-room, the end of a corridor, space underneath a hall stage might all offer temporary storage for work in progress, or completed work which is not required until the end-of-project display. In such cases it is often advisable to put such work in boxes to prevent damage, or cover it with newspaper to avoid soiling. Often last minute repairs or touching-up may be necessary, but such precautions should prevent the distress which can result from work being carelessly pushed on top of a cupboard for a few weeks without any warning notices, and children having too little time to repair the ensuing damage.

As well as some form of exhibition at the end of a project, children in the class will be pleased to see finished work on display, and as the project proceeds some space will have to be allotted for this purpose.

In addition to a record book of class work planned and achieved, it is a sensible idea to keep a project file in which aspects affecting organization are recorded week by week, to take account of the developing state of the project, as well as activities which will require special attention: e.g. use of a special room in the school for film or television viewing; use of the hall for some associated drama or movement work; an early lunch to enable the children to go out for an afternoon of fieldwork, etc.

The creativity and dynamism of the project are the features which make it exciting; it is the underlying organization which makes it work. If forward planning is applied to the latter, more time and attention can be given to the former.

Much of the organization within the classroom may be dependent upon the cooperation of other people, particularly colleagues with special responsibility for library/resources, environmental studies, general stock, etc., and discussion at an early stage with them will create not only goodwill but also produce the materials or services required. The rapport built up will also help when a real emergency arises. Where there is going to be a lot of creative work to be completed, for example, as the class moves towards an exhibition deadline, a word in advance to the cleaner should ensure that the classroom can be safely left overnight, and that teacher will not be met with a deputation of the headteacher, the caretaker and his cleaning staff the following morning.

A teacher can learn a great deal by observing and talking with a colleague about the skills of organization which have been learnt through experience. To ask a colleague whose methods and approach you admire – 'How do you make sure the children understand what they have to do when you are busy with one group? What do you suggest I do if the enthusiasm and work which is coming from the project means that we are going to over-run the half term? Who would you suggest I should invite to accompany me on the first excursion?' – is likely to save a great deal of time and frustration, and gain a friend.

The important thing with advice is to listen and see how it will fit a particular situation. If it doesn't, but is still valuable, modify it to suit the circumstances – including teaching style, the particular children, the constraints of the room, etc.

Introducing the Project

Part of the planning of a project should include a careful consideration of how best to launch it. Matters which might affect the choice of overture are: the class – numbers, ages, abilities, potential; whether the teacher has worked with the class before – and in this way; how the children have responded to various kinds of introduction; the particular project.

The opening phase of the project needs to be carefully handled. If the class senses that the teacher is uneasy working outside the usual formal structure the children may take advantage of the situation by mistaking a new approach as a sign of relaxation of control. If, however, relationships are well developed, then the teacher can adopt an unconventional beginning. Obviously there must be a direct link between the introduction and the follow-up, and the project as a whole. Similarly the initial stimulus, however well thought out, will be wasted if the remainder of the work is not adequately planned. A later section (p. 62) discusses different approaches to project work, and the choice of introduction should be related to this. Where the children are accustomed to working with a teacher in this particular way, they will assume that at various times during the year, a new project will get under way. If project work is a new departure then greater care may be required. Advance publicity is a good ploy, because it raises anticipation about what might be ahead. So the announcement could be:

'Tomorrow I'm going to tell you about this term's project.'
'At the end of the afternoon I'm going to introduce our special study project. I think you'll find it very interesting because it links with work we did last term/is something rather new and special for you/is what we were discussing as a possibility after our visit to the airport.'
'Next week, we begin the Spring Term project. Over the weekend could you look around and see if you could find out/By Monday could you ask your parents, how many of them can lend us/tell us/come in to . . .'

The time arranged for the announcement should be kept to, and the details must live up to the promise – a let-down at this stage can deliver a body blow from which the project and the class never recover.

Of course the whole project can begin in low key, with a simple statement about the theme which is going to be followed and what the children are going to do individually, in groups and as a class. Key events, particularly those which have already been programmed, can be announced. While this session may be a matter-of-fact occasion, it can be conducted with directness and enthusiasm.

Introduction can take many forms, and some suggestions are listed below. Most can be adapted to suit circumstances; others can be amalgamated.

1   A film or TV programme which provides an attractive and informative overview or introduction to the project area, or part of it.
2   An educational radio or radio-vision programme which fulfils the

same purpose as 1. Subsequent discussion about the programmes should draw out many of the issues which the children identify as important.

3   An attractive classroom display of pictures, photographs and objects in which attention is focused on the project. Time to arrange such a display is necessary. With forward planning this can be done on the evening before the project is due to start; in schools where teachers come into school before the end of the holiday, a day could be set aside for setting up a stimulating display.

4   A more modest corner or wall display which contains items of special interest to examine or to experiment with or to use in some other way.

5   A lead lesson with appropriate illustrations – posters, slides or overhead-projector transparencies – sound effects, music or recorded conversation on tape to outline the main points of the forthcoming project.

6   A talk by an expert to set the scene. The expert may be a member of a teaching team, someone else on the staff, a specialist from outside, e.g. an adviser, a colleague in another school, a layman.

7   A discussion to produce two lists headed: *What We Know About. What We do not Know About.* The list could provide some useful guidelines on areas to focus upon. The inexperienced teacher may find the announcement of a project greeted with calls of 'We've done that'. If this is true, the teacher is at fault for not finding this out and avoiding the repetition; if the teacher does know and intends to take the class on from there, the completion of the two lists should establish for both teacher and class the present state of knowledge.

8   The reading of a first stimulating chapter of a story which will be part of the literature component of the project.

9   Show and talk about one unusual object from the project. For example:

> 'Now this might look just like an ordinary piece of metal, but in fact it is . . .'
> 'Would it surprise you to know that this article I have in my hands is just over 100 years old? Can you suggest what it might have been used for by your great, great-grandmother?'
> 'I've borrowed this from the local museum. It's a case of things found in this area last year when they were building the new . . .'

Hopefully the class will respond with a variety of answers and so the first session becomes a stimulating start to the whole venture.

10   Produce a simple flow-chart and invite the children to propose other associations, thus gaining greater commitment.

11   A visit of introduction (e.g. to a market town, a church, a museum, an exhibition) in which the main aim is to stimulate interest and gather

impressions, to be followed as soon as possible by a discussion on what lines of enquiry could be fruitfully followed.

12   Turn the classroom into a time machine, the children into space travellers and encourage them to anticipate what they might see as they journey through time, or space.

13   A box of old postcards or newspaper cuttings to start the children off talking, conjecturing and deciding how they would go about finding out more.

14   An invitation to someone, or a special group who are visiting the area, to visit the school.

Virgil advised us to 'Be favourable to Bold Beginnings' and if a bold beginning can be planned and executed well, then the project takes off in top gear.

Activities and Experiences Inside the School

The classroom is the working base for the project and so should be an attractive and interesting place. The teacher will be educating the children in a variety of ways by what is arranged, how, why, where and for how long. Children too, stimulated by the project, will respond to invitations to bring things into the class. Some objects will be there to be looked at, others to be examined and hopefully still more to be used. But unless such objects are particularly striking some, if not all, of the children may miss the display or give it little more than a cursory glance. The teacher can draw attention to a display by labelling the material boldly or by putting a written question or a suggestion for some associated work alongside it. For greater effect the teacher should refer to a new display, speak about its significance, and involve the children in talking about it and how the objects might be used. Children soon fall into a routine and willingly respond to a request to 'Watch This Space'.

Through workcards, children can be directed to carry out a number of activities. As the teacher moves around the classroom or the children come up to the teacher's table, they can be encouraged to talk about their experiences and say what they have learnt. The conversation may enable the teacher to prompt a child to try out something else linked with the project.

It cannot be assumed that children know how to set out an account of an experiment; the following pattern or framework may help them order their material:

A   What I had to find out:
B   What I needed to carry out the work:
C   What I did: (set out in sequential steps)
D   What happened:
E   What I learned:

The teacher going over the work needs to question the child about the activity. Depending upon circumstances the teacher may take the pupil through a particular line of thought and then persuade the child to go forward alone. The sequence of events might go as follows:

1   Note an important feature, e.g. something unresolved; something which is unexpected; something which doesn't conform to the pattern.
2   Consider why this should be so.
3   Search for further information and ideas.
4   Plan for further work.
5   Repeat in a different way.
6   Note whether a pattern is occurring.
7   What conclusions can now be reached?
8   Can the results be tested?
9   What have we found out?
10 Can we go further?

Obviously this process can be used by a small group as well as by an individual. Indeed the work would be improved because of the inter-action of members of the team. If a leader emerges so much the better. Of course the teacher must still know when and how best to intervene. Children do need guiding when first learning a particular method of investigation but as soon as possible the teacher should be encouraging the children to determine their own questions and means of solving the problems they are investigating.

There will probably be various planned experiences during the project which are important for all the children, e.g. a film or other audio-visual aid experience, the reading of a story related to the work in hand, a discussion following an excursion. These and similar occasions will often give rise to work which may be the same for everyone, suggestions from which the children might select, or a personal choice about follow-up work. Similarly, it may be that the response is a communal one, e.g. drama or movement work; or groups of children doing similar activities, e.g. a frieze or decorative appliqué wall-hanging; or groups opting for different occupations, e.g. a musical composition, 3-D modelling, a play production, a presentation using slides and taped commentary, a series of interviews, and so on.

In the latter case, where a variety of tasks is being pursued in different places and with a variety of resources, a great deal of forward planning and discussion with the children will have to take place. Only a well-organized and confident teacher, working with a class already quite experienced in such sophisticated autonomous methods of working, should attempt to operate on such an ambitious scale. A narrower base might be better for a less-experienced teacher; or perhaps there should only be such a wide range of activities when extra, well-briefed, competent help is available.

Part of the discussion with a group must cover the actual part which each member of the team will play, so that as far as possible everyone is involved for as much of the time as possible, and individuals, and indeed groups, know what tasks they will move onto when they have completed that particular assignment. There is no way in which every group will finish its work simultaneously and so this contingency must be prepared for. It may be that some groups will wish to continue in their own time —·during breaks or after school. If this is possible, they must be supervised. Parts of the project may need to be taken home for further work. Both responses are to be encouraged because of the enthusiasm they indicate.

Much has already been said about the importance of teacher planning. Opportunities for departures from the plan will regularly arise and, since they will frequently represent children's interest, it will be valuable to allow for this flexibility within the general framework of the study.

Throughout primary education the teacher will be striving for a correct balance of activities; and so within the project it will be important for the child to make a contribution to both class and group activities, and also to keep a personal file or workbook and carry out art and craft work on an individual basis.

In this section, it has been suggested that responses of all kinds should arise from a project. For instance there may be an intellectual response, in which the children engage in descriptive writing about TV programmes they have watched about 'new towns'; or there could be a creative response in which a group of children decide that they would like to design and plan a new settlement themselves, which would involve them in making a ground plan and building three-dimensional flats and houses on it; or they could develop a role-playing activity in which a group of new 'inhabitants' attend an enquiry at the 'Town Hall' to complain about the lack of amenities.

Just as it would be regrettable if the class did not have some experience of various forms of writing, so it is important that children have the opportunity to express themselves through design and craft activities, drama as well as singing and other creative forms of music making, painting and drawing. So in various ways their feelings about certain issues will find expression. It may be that the teacher has little talent for some of the arts but is anxious that the children should experience them. There may be someone on the staff who could demonstrate the techniques, observe a lesson and comment upon it constructively afterwards. The class would benefit if a specialist on the staff was asked to pursue a particular dimension of the project. If the alternative were no drama or movement work at all, then it may need some reorganization of the timetable to make it possible.

Although there are cutbacks in in-service training in some authorities, courses still exist for teachers who want workshop experience. Ideas also exist in books and educational magazines. It may be possible to be released to visit another school nearby where new ideas can be observed in practice, and discussed. There may be an LEA adviser who specializes in this subject area who, with the head's approval, could be invited in to talk and demonstrate. Where the type of work would be a departure from the school norm, it would be wiser for the teacher to explain to the head just what work is envisaged and to seek approval. It is better to start rather modestly, discuss the activity with the children, and explain the limits of action. It is surprising how stimulating an unexpected experiment which is well-planned can be.

Resources Inside the School

The planning of the project will include a consideration of available resources. The quantity, quality and variety of resources can have a direct effect upon the project; the way in which they are made available, phased in and out, and used by the children will affect their degree of interest in, as well as understanding of, the project.

Printed resources
Print will be the predominant resource. Most primary schools have a library or central collection of books in some form or other. It is helpful not only for the present needs of the children but also for their future requirements to have some form of book classification, e.g. Dewey, preceded by colour coding for lower-primary children. A catalogue needs to be available, if possible complemented by a wall display of the main subjects covered with their classification alongside, so that books can be found easily. The wall catalogue should enable new projects to be slotted in alphabetically. All arrangements in a library should be as simple as possible. If a ticket-dating system can be dispensed with, so much the better. Where children are to be encouraged to take books home to continue their studies then the teacher concerned can make a brief note of this arrangement without involving the overworked teacher-librarian.

Ancillary workers, volunteer parents and older children can do much of the administrative work of the library, with the teacher as overseer dealing with those who ignore the procedures or the privileges, arranging attractive displays, promoting new books, and winning colleagues' cooperation.

Over a period of time, the teacher-librarian will know the stock and will be an important person with whom to discuss suitable project resources. This knowledge should extend to stories which provide both stimulus and valuable information in a very palatable form.

In addition to the central collection of books, there will probably be others in different parts of the school, especially in the classroom, and it should be possible to draw upon these too.

When the chosen project is likely to be repeated in future years, the librarian will be pleased to have recommendations for suitable new books for the school. Whoever is recommending books should have examined them at an exhibition or elsewhere, and be satisfied that they meet a set of criteria relating to accuracy of information, up-to-date subject matter, interesting and related illustrations, suitable reading age for primary school children, stimulating approach, good index, general attractiveness and durability of binding. The price of the book and value for money must also be an important consideration today.

Many LEAs operate a loan scheme as do county public libraries. As with so many other aspects of project work, advance warning will ensure a better service. Specific titles can be mentioned, but experienced librarians are usually happy to be given the age-group of the children and the title of the project, providing this is not a global theme like 'Mankind'.

In addition, use can be made of booklets, leaflets, press cuttings and illustrations collected from a variety of sources. How to store such items can cause problems for the school librarian. Where such print resources arise in large quantities, strong boxes can be used to hold together those items linked with a particular theme, and the usual cataloguing and classification systems can be employed.

Similar solutions have to be found when the resources diversify further. Where audio tapes, slides, filmstrips, overhead-projector trans-parencies, actual objects and samples are used, these should ideally be shelved near books on the same subject. Some schools have made space now available as a result of falling rolls into multi-media resource centres. Some authorities are able to make short-term loans of exhibits through a museum service. The only problem with such services is that demand exceeds supply and booking must be several months ahead of the project dates.

Schools are increasing the flexibility of their TV viewing by purchasing video-cassette recorders. Many possess a 16mm projector (or can borrow one from the LEA) and so show films – once again ordered well in advance.

The use of a variety of media gives much greater impact to the project. Where the children are able to use the hardware themselves, this will increase their motivation. The teacher too must feel confident about using an Elf projector or VCR. Short practical courses can usually be arranged to provide the necessary expertise.

Such diversification of supporting materials requires management. This will include the development of a system, and once this is devised, then the teacher can delegate responsibility to a group of children who can ensure the smooth running of the whole operation – providing they have been trained.

As part of the preparation, the teacher can draw up a resources plan (see Fig. 8, p. 36) whose range, quality, availability and quantity of categories will determine the direction, interest and success of the project. Since books and other printed material are likely to predominate, it would help the teacher compiling the resources planning-list to allow more space for them than is given in this example. Where some items are only available for a short period of time, or can only be used when particular equipment, working spaces or operators are available, then this information can be noted in the planning schedule, and crossreferenced with the master plan.

Where space is at a premium, and to take account of the boredom which can arise through over-familiarity, if the project can be divided into a number of distinct phases, many resources can be phased in and out (and possibly in again later). This policy should be quite deliberate and apply to wall charts and other materials in use. This gives the project a sense of urgency and most children will respond by seeking out the things they need in plenty of time.

We must not forget that school colleagues are resources! All of them could probably surprise us with their talents, skills, knowledge and experience, so it is important to let them know what project is under way. In some schools, the work of each class is well-known. In other cases the teacher may have to seek out colleagues and explain what is needed. All contacts and links will help, from experienced fellow teachers to colleagues on a course or at the local teachers' centre.

We are frequently reminded that most writing which people engage in after they have completed formal schooling, will be in the form of letters. Opportunities to learn and practise the art of letter-writing will occur during a project – an obvious example is the request for information or material. The teacher should always look over the letters to ensure that they are legible, comprehensible, correctly set out and addressed, and, if requests are being made, reasonable. A covering letter from the teacher on the school-headed notepaper would probably be advisable, especially where the recipient is not one of the institutions which advertise their educational facilities. A few years ago a reminder was sent to London schools suggesting that letters sent to the West

Figure 8   A project resource plan

Resources	In possession	In school – available	Can be produced in school with assistance	without assistance	Teachers' centre loan	Can be produced at teachers' centre – with assistance	without assistance	LEA loan	National loan	Authority to purchase/hire
Reference books										
Story books										
Booklets/pamphlets										
Newspaper cuttings										
Picture material										
Maps/plans										
Charts										
Information packs										
Records										
Audio tapes										
Audio cassettes										
Tape/slide material										
Radio-vision materials										
OHP transparencies										
Slide sets										
Filmstrips										
8mm film loops										
8mm films										
16mm films										
Video tapes										
Video cassettes										
Multi-media kits										
Realia										
Other materials										

German Embassy asking for information about Hitler were perhaps not in the best taste. So the teacher may need to act as censor occasionally.

From time to time over the years I have used correspondence as an important stimulus and resource for the children. As with so many other aspects of the project, arrangements have to be made beforehand. A New Zealand project was much enhanced by the exchange of letters with a school on the other side of the world. A project on Forestry was made particularly interesting by the correspondence which developed with a Hertfordshire school, which had a forest plot, and whose children were doing a parallel project on trees themselves; the children acted as hosts for our class visit.

School journeys provide opportunities for concentrated educational and social experiences. They can, however, deteriorate into the annual tour of all the regular tourist attractions in a particular area. Where the same staff have been in charge of the arrangements for a decade or so, then the visit to this stately home, that castle, and the bird reserve on the same day each year must lose some of its shine. Too frequently the party has little contact with the people of the area. On a number of occasions, contact with the local school (an exploratory letter to the County Education Authority should provide an accommodating head-teacher) has brought forth a pen-pal system which has gone on throughout the preparation (and later). From my own experience of this in Swanage, Conway and a Scottish village, I felt that the visiting children knew a great deal more about the region they were to visit because of the interchange letters.

Letters as resources have also featured in the 3Fs of environmental education – farming, forestry and fishing. The work of the Association of Agriculture is well known. One of their services is to provide sample studies of particular farms in different parts of the world on a subscription basis. Over the years various ideas have been employed and at the time when I used the service, I enjoyed the letter which came out regularly to report on activities on the various farms. There was little opportunity to visit or correspond with these farmers because of the number of schools who used the service. I felt therefore that it would be useful to establish personal links with a farmer. Our school staff included the daughter of a farmer, the friend of a farmer, and one of the pupil's was a farmer's nephew. Each was asked to see whether correspondence was possible. All three responded positively and so we had available in class a number of letters from people who farmed in different parts of the country. The class concentrated upon the second contact for three reasons: the farm was nearer to the school than the others; it was run by a woman; the farmer agreed to sustain a correspondence over twelve months. (In fact this ran to two years, and two different groups of children benefited from an Ambridge-type serial of various events on the farm – the arrival of the milking machine, the birth of a calf, buying and selling animals, foodstuff and machinery at the local market, etc.) Examples of these letters can be seen in the National Dairy Council publication *The Class, The Cow and the Bottle on the Doorstep*.

In a similar way, a class making a study of trees in their local park (where incidentally there was a greater variety of trees than in many parts of the countryside) were able to hear once a month from a Sussex forester about the changing seasons and how they affected his work. One of the difficulties facing a teacher carrying out a study over twelve months is to maintain interest. This can be achieved by the regular introduction of new features, activities, resources, etc. The arrival of the forester's letter always brought a new wave of interest. The letter was duplicated and a copy given to each child, who in turn wrote back telling their friend in the South Down forest what they had been doing, and asking for information, which he dutifully provided.

Both this forester and the farmer were able to come to London to visit the class during the project and in turn invited us to visit them. (A fuller account of the forestry project can be found in the Forestry Commission's booklet *Forestry and the Town School*.)

For the fishing project, extending over a term, we made contacts through coastguards, lifeboat secretaries and harbour masters. The 'catch' was some ten fishermen who wrote to the children and described the way they went to sea to harvest the fish. The letters included drawings, photographs and dramatic descriptions of the difficulties of their trade. Most amazing of all was the very long letter from a former whaling captain who spoke of all kinds of adventures in the ice in Arctic waters. Apart from learning a great deal about the particular projects they were engaged in, the children learnt something of the art and convention of letter-writing in a far more exciting way than if they had been engaged in a sterile exercise from a textbook.

Resources must include materials which can aid identification – be it of a bird in flight, a winter bud, an architectural feature or a fossil – and which give children the opportunity to develop their skills in using keys. It is well worth spending a little more to buy the best possible reference books which give a variety of examples. All too often the example children see 'in the field' is nothing like the perfect specimen illustrated in the book.

Similarly it should be possible for children to practise in advance skills such as making a plaster casting or brass rubbing. Descriptions of how to go about such activities can be included in the resources, as can the opportunity to carry them out. For example, in the case of the casting, impressions could be made in clay and plaster poured in after a collar of card or old lino had been placed in position. One classroom recently visited had a deer's foot which was used to make an impression in clay. Various things can be used to practise 'rubbing' in class, but it may be possible to visit the various brass rubbing centres in some towns and cities before starting such work in a church.

Workcards

Workcards perform a number of useful functions:

1 They provide a form of control over the work of the class, i.e. a substitute teacher.
2 They keep children occupied. The important thing is to ensure that the children are profitably occupied.
3 They provide a structure to the work and enable the child to learn how to learn, including how to set out responses.
4 They enable the teacher to circulate among the children.
5 Children are able to work at their own pace. The teacher can colour-code cards of similar levels of difficulty, so that children can be directed towards those most appropriate to their needs and stage of development. Alternatively, coding can be used to indicate aspects of the project, so ensuring that children are introduced to different features of the study.
6 The teacher is freed from the role of instructor. General as well as particular intructions can be provided succinctly on the workcard.
7 Workcards give children access to information presented at the right level and in an appropriate format.
8 They can provide a variety of approaches and stimulation which should make the children want to use them.
9 Their use should accelerate the process of developing independent learning in the pupils. This implies careful planning of workcards to help the children progress towards increasing responsibility for their own education.

There are a number of practical educational points to keep in mind when devising workcards.

The very youngest children, and those who have not made a confident start in reading whatever their age, must be accommodated, and so the scope for printed text and written response will be more limited. The strategies used by infant teachers and remedial teachers to assist such children can be employed, e.g. plentiful illustrations; familiar levels and forms of language; assistance from more competent readers. The level of conceptual development and the various skills should be acknowledged, and workcards made appropriately demanding and sophisticated. For the less fluent children it may be appropriate to read out the information and instructions to be followed. Every teacher should give general instructions orally on how the children are to use the workcards.

So often the children, when changing from one class to another, find themselves expected to work in an entirely different way. It is incumbent upon each teacher to make a new approach clear to the children. If the work prescribed on the workcards is to be regarded as important, then the teacher should keep a record of the workcards in use, and devise some system of checking who is working on which card; which cards have been checked and discussed with the children; and which ones are currently in use. Such a monitoring system will provide the teacher with information about the popularity of some cards, the ease or difficulty with which children are tackling them, the demand for more cards on the same subject matter but at different levels of ability, the need for further or different resources (or possibly more assistance in using them). The pupils will be aware of the teacher's monitoring and be more attentive both to the details of the procedures and their application.

It is important to consider a number of further points when compiling workcards.

1   Why has this particular mode of learning been employed? Have other more successful means been considered?
2   Is it clear what the children have to do and find out? What are the key facts, concepts or skills which are being developed?
3   Have we listed all the resources which the children will require? Have we pointed out the type and location of unusual or unfamiliar items? (With older children accustomed to working in this way such help may not be required; for younger children it will be necessary to direct children towards either the index, chapter, page or paragraph.) Are all the resources listed available?
4   Is it clear how and where the children should put their answers, observations, impressions, ideas? Are these usually limited to writing and drawing?
5   Do the cards invite the children to use as many of their senses as possible? (Usually the children are limited to looking at print and pictures in a fact-finding exercise!)
6   Do the cards encourage the use of a number of sources and of different types?
7   Are the instructions related to practical work given in clear sequential order? If the child is told exactly what to do, even to the extent of being told what the result will be, then such activity could hardly be described as discovery learning. Rather than ask one question, it may be preferable to devise sequential questions which take the child along in a series of short steps. Thus the child should be able to extract the important ideas, understand and interpret them and work through the card at a steady pace.
8   Wherever possible open-ended questions should be included to

enable the children to use and develop their thinking and imaginative powers. This will particularly apply to the most able children.

9   Is the language lively? Can the children understand it easily? Are the drawings and diagrams accurate, clear, labelled and necessary? Is there a good balance between text and illustration?

10   Has enough time been allotted to complete the card? One card may ask too many questions; some questions may be duplicated, some could be eliminated for other reasons. It may be preferable to produce two or more cards on particular facets of a subject if it is not possible to reduce the number of questions.

11   Are some questions too general? 'Find out all you can about North America' might be regarded as an extreme example!

12   The aesthetic appeal of the card should receive adequate attention. The use of colour, underlining, symbols, etc., should be used to emphasize particular aspects. Pictures, where used, should be cut out, trimmed and mounted with care. Writing can be applied directly to the card (faint pencil guidelines will help to keep it neat). If the teacher's handwriting is poor, then typewritten texts can be prepared and mounted with a spray adhesive. Lamination will add a few pence to the cost of a card but will make it more durable and keep it in mint condition for much longer. Obviously all the necessary information, coding, etc., has to be applied, and any pencilled guidelines removed, before lamination. Some teachers' centres have laminating machines which produce a very good finish, but for these a thinner manilla card must be used.

Well-produced workcards represent a useful long-term resource for the class and school. In such cases there is a virtue in producing material on standard sized cards which could then be stored and retrieved more easily. Incidentally, it may be preferable for the illustrations and a certain amount of basic text to be permanently protected under Celofilm, and for the teacher to write additional data and/or questions on top, using a spirit-based OHP or felt pen. This information can later be erased using a suitable solvent such as methylated spirits.

There are series of commercially-produced workcards on the market and usually these are well produced. They may, and often do, fall short of the ideal in other respects. Of major importance is the fact that they are not tailored to meet the needs of particular children, of a particular school or even a particular area. (Some sets of cards are exempt from such criticism because their subject matter has a universal application, e.g. Macmillan's large kit on *The Sea*.) A local authority may involve individuals or groups of teachers in producing materials for use as workcards and resource materials. Some years ago I was involved at two levels in devising such cards. The River Thames is an important educational resource for London schools and a number of resource packs were prepared for both teachers and their pupils. ILEA were able to take the basic materials, which had been tried in various schools, and produce these professionally and sell them at competitive prices. At a more modest level, a group of teachers studied the substantial ruins of an Augustinian Abbey, which is visited by many schools in the Woolwich area. There was an obvious need for background material for teachers and worksheets for children. The local teachers' centre designed a work booklet and charged for little more than the paper.

The workcard is closely associated with worksheets used on educational visits and there are certain features common to both. Particular forms of instruction and questioning are employed both to direct observations and structure the process of thinking and other more practical activities. Thus we may ask the children to *classify* various observations, or *estimate or calculate* the quantities, or to *recall* something from memory ('Write down the names of . . .'), or to *interpret* some phenomena observed or *apply* some knowledge.and understanding ('Can you suggest some things which could be made from . . .?').

It is a salutary experience to ask a colleague to look critically at one's workcards. At various teachers' workshops workcards have been exchanged and worked through – sometimes with great difficulty! The main aim of the workcard is to assist the children to learn. Not all do.

Educational Visits

'In the classroom the most helpful aid is the window, and the most helpful piece of equipment is the door' (Ken Hoy, Warden of 'Suntrap', Waltham Forest Centre). We need to take our children out of the classroom to add a special significance and dimension to the project. There will be few projects which do not benefit from outside observation and other activities.

But the teacher needs to consider certain questions in order to be able to justify such work:

Why take children outside the school to learn?
Have the objectives for the visit been clearly established?
Is this particular visit the best way to achieve the desired goals?
Will the educational and social gains justify the amount of time spent?
Will the excursion create problems for the school in terms of the education and supervision of those children left behind?

The venue for the visit should be chosen with care. A well-known example may spring to mind, but it may be possible to choose a site which is nearer school and less crowded which will provide the same educational opportunities. It is important not to overtire the children, or allow the journey itself to take up the major part of the day.

Frequently parents will be invited to contribute towards part, if not all, of the cost of travel. Schools usually make special provision for those children who are unable to make a full contribution. There may be a school minibus or parents can often be persuaded to ferry children in private cars if the distance is not excessive. Local authorities normally have regulations relating to this type of transport and these must be adhered to; parent-drivers should be asked to check with their insurance companies to ensure that they have adequate cover.

Education authorities make the question of safety on outings the subject of a policy statement and this will state in unequivocal terms the minimum number and status of adult supervision which must be available. This will be related to the age of the pupils and the nature of the visit. Schools may prefer to increase this cover if the type of activity or the venue demands it. Parents, governors and ancillary workers can be invited to accompany and supervise the party, but must have clear instructions on what they are required to do. The more advance warning all concerned can have the better – three or four weeks should be possible in most cases, with adequate forethought. Parents who are going to be asked to give their financial support to the venture will need this kind of notice and possibly the opportunity to pay by instalments. In any case, there must be no discrimination against pupils on the ground of cost. The school fund should be available for this type of contingency.

Communications with parents

Parents need to be informed about the visit, and indeed to give their approval for their child to go. Those parents whose first language is not English will require special attention. The new teacher may like to use the standard form of letter used by the school on these occasions. It will be important to include all relevant information from the following checklist:

Day, date and departure time from the school.
Venue, and brief reason for visit, and its relation to the project being studied.
Information relating to food, drink and type of container (e.g. no glass bottles).
Request relating to contributions towards the costs of the day – travel, entrance fees, etc.
Suggestions and limits relating to other money which the children might bring, and how this might be used, e.g. to buy a hot drink at the destination, postcards or guidebooks.

Instructions on appropriate clothing and footwear, for both the weather and the type of activity to be carried out.

Whether volunteer parental help would be appreciated.

Estimated time of arrival back in school.

It is often more helpful in the long run to include many of these suggestions as instructions, thus avoiding ambiguity, or the possibility of children applying pressure on their parents to override a sensible proposal from school, e.g. that no drink is to be carried in glass bottles. The language used can be firm without being officious. Where it is imperative to have parents exercise their options because a feature of a visit could offend on religious or ethnic grounds, matters must be expressed clearly. Where particular children are poor travellers, it seems a wise precaution for appropriate medicine or tablets to be administered, but this should always be with the agreement of the family doctor.

There are often opportunities for children to take photographs, and while the teacher should indicate the value of this, it will be important for the parent to be reminded that children must be responsible for the care, protection and use of their own cameras (preferably already loaded with film), or binoculars or other valuable personal possessions. Some schools invite the parents to sign an indemnity clause so that they assume responsibility for their child's safety. The signing of such a statement does not remove or even reduce the normal statutory obligation on the teacher to provide reasonable care and attention, nor does it offer any protection if in the event of an accident the teacher was shown to be negligent in or out of normal school hours. Where a teacher feels unable to take responsibility for a particular child (or children) then the circumstances should be explained to the head and the parents as well as the child. In certain circumstances the parent of the child in question could be invited to accompany the visit, or another teacher in the party might be willing to assume responsibility.

It is obviously important for the headteacher to know exactly what is involved in any proposed visit and to make any additional recommendations which seem necessary. These might include suggestions on accompanying teachers, comments upon the suitability of the set tasks, reminders about other things to do before, during and after an excursion. Obviously the head will want to consider the overall effect of the visit on the efficient running of the school. Some local authorities insist upon being advised about any proposed visits and giving necessary clearance. Such rulings will extend the amount of time which will elapse between intention, planning and the actual excursion.

Other people in the school may be directly and indirectly involved in any excursion or activity which changes normal routine and the school may find it useful to compose an *aide-mémoire* which can be used during each project where a visit is envisaged. All manner of things which can go wrong will do so unless careful preparation is made; forward planning will eliminate most of them. The following sheet, modified to suit a particular school, could be duplicated and used on each occasion.

Some schools place limits on the number of visits which can be made by any one class and in any one week because of the disruptions which can occur.

Figure 9

Educational Visit Proforma   Approved by head ....

Approved by LEA ....

Visit venue(s) ....

Class ....   Dates ....

Teacher in charge .... Teachers accompanying ....

Other adults involved ....

Letter to parents with details ...... Duplicated ..... Despatched .....

Secretary informed .... Acknowledged ....

Cook informed ....

Other teachers associated with
the class on that day informed ....

Other classes affected by absence of
teachers on this excursion informed ....

Other effects on the school adjusted for Duties ..... Assemblies .....

Clubs ....

Transport required .... Booked .... Confirmed ....

Route to be used ....

Planned stops ....

Arrangements at venue ....

Facilities available on day of visit ....

Names of people involved ....

Services being provided by them .... Confirmed ....

Telephone numbers ....

Worksheets prepared .... Duplicated ....

Equipment required .... Booked ....

Looked out .... Taken .... Returned ....

Other materials ....

Prepared .... Taken ....

First-aid materials ....

Arrangements for meals ....

Toilet provision en route .... at venue ....

Costings

Transport .... Entrance fees .... Other charges ....

Total .... Charge per head ....

Cash received and balance sheet prepared ....

Teacher preparation

> Nothing is more miserable or more profitless than the day in the country in which the teacher tries to lead along a route he does not know, through a country of which he is ignorant, a group of children being given nothing to do but walk.
>
> *(Shave and Briault 1967)*

The teacher must make a preliminary reconnoitre of the place the class is to visit. It is much easier to help children find things if you know these items are there.

The teacher must attempt to gather all the relevant information, including printed data, to help prepare the children effectively, and perhaps to produce a worksheet. It is important to go over the complete route be it museum, galleries, the environs of a cathedral, or a town trail. The teacher should look for particular points of interest where it will be appropriate and convenient to stop, note suitable and varied activities for the children to engage in, as well as anticipate hazards and other difficulties which might arise. The height of items to be examined, the problems of thirty or more children trying to see things at the same time (it may be necessary to split the party at this point), the adequacy of labelling (where relevant), are all features which experienced teachers will note.

It will be important to meet in advance any guides or hosts, not only to establish social contact but also to confirm the purpose of the visit and tactfully suggest the kind of approach which will be most effective with a particular group of children given the extent of their present knowledge of the subject. In certain situations where a guide has what appears to be a memorized commentary from which he or she is unable to diverge, this may be satisfactory for the school party. But if it is not, it would be better for the teacher to 'take in' the official version and edit it for the children's use. This might include a modification of the route, which may or may not be permitted.

Class preparation

Anthony Jarvis, owner of Doddington Hall in Lincolnshire, put the point neatly in the *Guardian* (6.2.79) when he said, 'Without preparation, school parties waste most of their time and all of ours.' Children do need careful briefing if they are to gain much from their experiences out-of-doors. If the visit takes place in the middle or near the end of the project, then the children should already possess a lot of information relating to the central theme, and should therefore be able to gain much from the day. Nevertheless the class will require a planned introduction to the proposed order of events for the day, with information on who they will meet and what they can expect to see and do. There should always be the opportunity to ask questions to clarify matters at this briefing session. Wherever possible all the adults accompanying the excursion should also attend this preliminary meeting. Where a parent or a teacher is not able to do so, then a duplicated sheet of instructions and details should be provided, including names of particular children in particular groups and special assignments which may have been allotted or chosen. (In any case such a printed summary would be a useful reminder sheet for all concerned.)

Where the excursion is being used to introduce the whole project, then the preparation must be just as detailed, and the children given more indication of what they might see, so that they can gather a variety of impressions which can be discussed afterwards.

Worksheets are frequently employed with older children. They can represent a useful checklist of items which the group is to see, inviting the children to give evidence of observation by writing in the spaces provided. The questions should invite observation of particular items in, say, a museum case, and not just involve copying an answer from the label. As many of the questions as possible should be open-ended and invite some thought and speculation. With the facilities which some schools and teachers' centres now have at their disposal quite handsome worksheets or booklets can be prepared. There is no reason why pairs of children or even larger groups cannot work together on an assignment sheet. The group itself can be asked to devise its own questions. In two schools visited recently the teacher of a first-year class invited the children to discuss the kinds of questions which they would ask the police officers they were to visit in the local police station. Apart from some of the more predictable questions, they came up with:

'Why did you become a policeman?'
'What do you feel like when you catch a criminal?'
'What parts of the job do you not like to do?'
'Why are you called "bobbies"?'
'What happens when you find somebody dead?'
'Do you know where my dad is?'

A third-year group preparing for a visit to a church asked some equally interesting questions which the teacher put in the quiz sheet:

'Why has the church got this name?'
'Why was the church built there?'
'What materials were used in the building of the church and where did they come from?'
'What's it like being a vicar? What jobs do you do?'
'If you weren't a vicar what would you do?'
'Where do the names vicar and curate come from?'
'How tall is the spire?'
'How do they ring the bells?'

It will be important for the teacher to go over the worksheet with the children, particularly if some of them are not confident readers.

In many circumstances a map or plan is a useful tool to give the class and on the preliminary visits this may have to be prepared or a standard map modified and marked with the special features which the children are to look out for.

The class may have prepared a model of a castle or port they are to visit, and this too can be a useful aid for the briefing session. Sometimes other illustrations can be used to give the children a better idea of what they will be seeing, such as a series of slides purchased or taken personally on the preliminary visit, or a movie film made by a class who had been there on a previous excursion.

There may also be occasions when the host can be invited to come to the school before the visit to meet the party and introduce his or her farm, ship, factory or whatever.

The Day of the Excursion

The previous day (or the Friday if the visit is to be on a Monday) will have seen the children's preparation completed, and the gathering together, often in containers for easy movement to the coach or other transport, of all necessary items:

Educational equipment: which might include tape recorders, cameras, work-boards, measuring apparatus, containers for collecting items, reference books, spare paper, pencils, etc.
First aid equipment including pail, paper towels, disinfectant, aerosol spray in case of sickness.
Refreshments: Large container of orange squash and paper cups which can overcome the problem of children carrying their own drinks.
Box of reading matter in case the journey is long and/or tedious.

The departure time at the school should be emphasized at the briefing, especially if it is before the usual time for morning school. A time-limit for latecomers should be decided upon; a tactful but direct reminder to regular latecomers can usually pre-empt the difficulty. Where the coach does leave without the full complement of children, then the teacher in charge must make sure to leave a written note to that effect if it is an early morning departure, or to see the head directly. It is important to make an accurate count of the number of children in the party on departure to save any doubts during the day when regular tallies should be made, especially in busy areas, or where the party is split up for various tasks.

The leader of the visit will require a personal checklist to include lunch, rainwear, papers relating to the visit (including telephone numbers and names of people to be met).

The coach should be ready to leave on time. A phone call to the hiring company on the previous afternoon should help to ensure this, with confirmation of the route to be followed (if this is important) and the actual destination. It is not unknown for a driver to be unfamiliar with an area or a particular destination. If there is any doubt then the leader should sit at the front of the coach and map read. In the preparatory visit the teacher could note a coach park near the destination and be prepared to direct the driver to it. If time is lost at this stage of the day it can seriously disrupt the programme and possibly mean missing a gallery lesson at a museum, or a rendezvous with a forester, or other curtailment of the activities planned in a very tight schedule. On long journeys, stops en route should be agreed with the driver but they should not be prolonged, nor should overeating and excessive drinking be permitted.

General behaviour on the coach including moving about, touching of window controls, eating lunch at 9.15 am in the morning, litter and noise level will all have been spelled out at the briefing. The allocation of seats and choice of travelling companions can usually be left to the good sense of a well-ordered class. It may be necessary to move children who infringe any of the modest rules previously announced. Teachers are more likely to have a trouble-free ride if they select seats at the rear of the coach. On a train journey or double-decker bus then each section should be supervised.

On arrival it is often a good idea to calm the party down by going over the first part of the 'campaign' once again. During that time one of the teachers can go to inform the host that the party has arrived. Toilets may be required, and if the journey was a long one, it may be appropriate to take the planned lunch break.

It may be necessary to issue equipment or materials, or put on special items of clothing or footwear, and this should be done in a careful, orderly fashion, setting the tone for the day, and avoiding overexcitement. The day as far as possible should normally proceed as planned. However, there should be a degree of flexibility. This may mean some adjustment of time as one planned activity takes a shorter or, more likely, a longer time to complete; a number of children require more time to finish an assignment; an unexpected observation is made – the landing of a helicopter on a beach bringing in a rescue victim, the appearance of an ornamental fowl and its willingness to stay and be admired; the invitation to enter a building when it was simply being admired from outside; the chance to go behind the scenes after a stage performance, etc.

Obviously it is impossible to accommodate each particular enthusiasm, but there is a case for the children having a degree of freedom during part of the day, to pursue their own interests. The teacher's responsibility for the safety of the party is paramount here and so it is reasonable to enforce some sensible limits in terms of time, range of movement, children going off in pairs or groups but never alone, etc.

Activities

In *An Environmental Experience* I described the preparation and planning of a school journey which lasted for ten days. The book's subtitle is 'Observe and Record'. These are usually the basic activities of a visit, i.e. looking carefully at something and selecting a means of making a permanent record of the information or impressions gained. The latter could be anything — a series of tally marks representing the number of brick lorries which left the yard on their way to a building site; a data sheet of Daisy's milk yield after her first calf; a list of the exact measurements of the foundations of a ruined abbey; a landscape drawing of a castle high on a promontory above the river; a detailed sketch of the winding gear on the sluice gate of a canal; a series of illustrations of different African animals in the zoo. There may be opportunities to make rubbings of brasses, gravestones, coal-hole covers, or the barks of trees; or take plaster-casts of impressions left in the mud by an animal; or tape recording discussions or explanations or sound effects; or photograph a farm machine at work lifting potatoes, or the village street with everyone going about their business. The important thing is that there is variety, relevance and interest in the activity, that the children can carry out the operations following training and experience, and that the necessary materials have been brought. There will be some experiences which the teacher will want all the children to have, but others can be enjoyed by groups or individuals, in many cases offering choice within a number of options. Frequently hosts are happy to provide samples of items which the class have seen produced or used. Collections of other kinds can also be made as long as there is no infringement either of the law or of good conservation sense.

I will, however, include here an account of a visit which went wrong.

I was leaving when a school bus arrived and out poured about forty ten-year-olds from a Newcastle primary school. I'd been going round the site almost on my own, apart from a party of Danish visitors, as it was so early in the morning. The kids immediately took over, rushing for the museum. One know-all shouted that he knew where there was a Roman catapult but the two lady teachers said hold on, we're going round the site first. They groaned, but turned and raced for the foundations with the teachers yelling at them not to knock anything over.

The teachers gave little bits of lectures, mainly gleaned from bending down and peering quickly at the notice boards on each site, a trick known to all teachers everywhere.

'They're a B stream,' confided one teacher, realizing I was watching. 'Their reading's not so hot.'

They then raced for the next site, the granaries. 'That's where the Romans kept their grannies,' said the know-all in a loud voice to his classmates.

They were herded on to the temples where one teacher reminded them of the lesson she'd given about temples and mosaics. 'But there's nothing on the floor, Miss! You said the Romans had mosaics on all their floors.' They were genuinely shocked, staring at the beautifully manicured but absolutely bare grass inside the foundations of the temple walls.

'Now we'll go and look at a very good painting of the fort as it used to be,' said the teacher hurriedly. They all fought to get on the dais, pushing and shoving. It was the thing they obviously liked best about the site, then they rushed at last to the museum huts. It was the know-all's turn to be criticized. The catapult wasn't full size, the way the rest of them had imagined, just a little model. The girls were all taken with the brooches and ornaments, but their interest soon waned.

Altogether, they'd been round everything in about fifteen minutes, despite the teachers stretching it out. Both teachers said they wished there was something for the kids to get involved with, to touch or play with or try to work or get inside. Luckily, they'd had a stop at a sweet shop on the way there, a unanimous demand by every child, where they'd unloaded every last penny. They rushed to sit on the bus and out came the sherbet, lemonades, crisps and chocolates. It was the highlight of their visit. Twenty years ago, I felt much the same.

From *A Walk Along The Wall* – Hunter Davies
(Weidenfeld and Nicolson, 1974)

Recently a London school visited Northumberland and included the Roman Wall in their schedule of visits. They studied the fort of Vindolanda. While the purist may object to the reconstruction of part of the wall and the inclusion of full-size replicas of Roman weapons, the young history students must have obtained a much more accurate impression of what it was like on the northern frontier of the Empire nearly 2000 years ago.

But they went a step further by bringing with them from their London school, armour and weapons for the Roman soldiers, and other clothes for the marauding Picts. Northern bleakness was added to the drama being enacted by the onslaught of a torrential rainstorm driven by a wind which made it difficult for the children to stand up and they soon found themselves much more interested in keeping dry and warm than imagining what life was like for the army of occupation.

There are several points worth mentioning at this stage. Dressing up and role playing will feed the imagination on this sort of visit. Imaginative literature and poetry can also help to provide images – for example, Rosemary Sutcliff's *Eagle of the Ninth* and the poem 'Roman Wall Blues' by W. H. Auden would be suitable for older juniors. To read part of the story and the verses actually on the site would be a stimulating experience. Finally, wherever possible there ought to be wet-weather alternatives built into any excursion or a willingness to curtail the visit.

Where a child or a group would rather throw stones into the sea than search rockpools, or clamber over dangerous castle walls rather than sketch the portcullis, or describe the dead cat in the gutter rather than the exhibits in the Roman room at the museum, then the teacher must seriously ask whether the activity is appropriate for the particular children, whether preparation has been adequate, and the children sufficiently well supervised. On the latter point, a broadsheet was issued by the Dales National Park which provides guidelines on how a school visit might be enjoyed. In the section on 'Hints to Staff in Charge of a School Group', they had this to say:

> Please stay with your group. If a coach of youngsters is left to find its own amusement whilst the teacher goes elsewhere, village folk do notice. At best, they lose confidence in all teachers. At worst, damage is done or casualties occur which could be avoided by adequate supervision. Plan the day thoroughly. Aim to keep the group occupied all the time. Be vigilant – don't turn a blind eye if you see members of your party causing damage to walls, throwing stones over cliff tops or leaving litter. No doubt you will all see some litter about, but encourage a pride amongst your pupils; 'Don't lower yourself to the mental level of the moron who dropped it' is a good line to take.

Strong words it might be felt, but clearly with so many parties visiting Malham they had sufficient justification for speaking as they did. Incidentally within their leaflet they discouraged the interviewing of local inhabitants, because through 'overkill' some of the residents are feeding back distorted information! As a general comment, it is important to prepare properly for an interview and to build in a check on the kind of information gained from it.

Concluding the Project

The end of a project is important not simply because it is the culmination and climax of a lot of hard work, but because of other special opportunities it presents to the class and groups and individuals.

The conclusion can act as a summary of all that has been experienced, making clear how every aspect has contributed towards the success of the whole and has therefore been significant. It is a time for all concerned to feel a sense of achievement, especially since it provides the opportunity to communicate knowledge and results to others.

The conclusion needs to be considered even during the planning stage as well as throughout the project. It may take a variety of forms. It will require space not usually available in the classroom (especially if there is to be an invited audience), and therefore arrangements may have to be made well in advance for the use of additional areas such as the hall, corridors, library or foyer. An exhibition of work may be envisaged and it may be necessary to supplement the available tables and boards. Ends of term and year are occasions for presentations, and so the need for extra equipment should be anticipated as much as possible. The time and duration of such an exhibition must be planned in relation to other factors.

Since the project enables the class to work on new material in a new way, the teacher may also wish to complete the work in a different fashion. This may simply be a broad decision with the precise details to be worked out in the light of the quantity and quality of actual achievements, and after discussion with the children concerned.

Where a lot of art and craft work of various kinds has been produced, then an exhibition of two- and three-dimensional materials will make a colourful display. Where written work is on show, it may be advisable for the teacher to write out examples in a script size large enough to be read from a range of two or three yards or else it will have little impact. Where work books and folders are on display, pages with stories, poems, or descriptive accounts can be opened at the pages relevant to an adjacent model, appliqué picture, etc.

Children involved in particular aspects of a project can be placed on a duty rota to stay with parts of the exhibition and explain details to visitors, e.g. the particular point of their fishing harbour, the cut-away model of a factory, or the diorama of a beach.

The teacher planning an exhibition will find it useful to look at the various ways in which those who dress windows, arrange museum dislays, or mount large stands in Earls Court or the local town hall, do their work. Points to look for include the general layout, the suggested route through the exhibition, the labelling and other descriptive data including a handout, the height of items on display, establishment of a sense of unity, background details, eye-catching devices, the use of audio-visual aids, the fascination of live demonstrations, opportunities for visitors to participate, the impact of the entrance and exit and the use of attendants.

Shopkeepers and exhibitors are often generous with display material of all kinds. While it is important to include the making of life-size figures in craft, it is often possible to ask for a pensioned-off model from a draper's shop so that children in the class can add some suitable costume, whether it be a pirate's costume or an astronaut's pressure suit, to produce a dramatic centre piece.

It is worth drawing a scale plan of the exhibition area and taking time to work out with a group of children how best to display their work to the public. A visitors' timetable may be needed to meet the needs of children and staff from the school and others nearby, as well as parents and governors.

Where space is at a premium, some parts of the show can be placed in the foyer, or the resource centre, as well as in the main display area. Alongside this static exhibition, there may be slides or films, and since these require blacked-out conditions an adjacent area should be prepared with times of showings announced and honoured! Depending of course upon the age and experience of the children, little supervision should be required in the 'cinema', other than a check from time to time to ensure that all is going satisfactorily.

There may be many ways in which the children can be actively involved in the presentation. For instance a series of brief lectures can be planned. An overhead projector is a useful additional aid for this purpose since it compels attention. Children can produce very satisfactory illustrations and can learn to operate the machine with only a minimum of instruction. Schools possessing a heat-copying machine will be able to make quite sophisticated transparencies for this kind of presentation. Teams of children should be invited to plan and rehearse the way they wish to deliver their remarks. The teacher can check for audibility, accuracy and timing, and provide advice on how the talk might be improved. The use of the tape-recorder to provide background effects and interviews with appropriate illustrations can add another dimension to the project. Once again children can operate the tape recorder themselves, using a cue sheet prepared at rehearsal.

A group can act as a panel of experts and respond to questions from the floor. If a question box has been available since the beginning of the exhibition, team members will have had the chance to look up answers and discuss them. This is obviously important when someone wants statistical information.

It often happens that assembly is the time chosen to speak about a completed project. Obviously some projects are more suitable than others for presentation at such a time. Frequently, with the teacher's guidance, facets of the project which have a bearing on people's humanity to others can be highlighted.

A lot of time, energy and imagination go into mounting any form of display and the teacher should be generous in observations to the class about what they have achieved and about the reactions of visitors. It may be possible and desirable to keep some items from the display, but as this is often a matter of sentiment, some photographs and tape recordings may suffice. The local press are always interested in special school events and will often respond to an invitation to attend the presentation of a project or other special occasions within it. Photographs and a short report are often then available for the school archives. Children should have the opportunity to take home not only their work folders but also items made in art, craft or fabric work.

This aspect of the project will have provided a variety of opportunities for children to take part in the important business of communication. It should be possible to involve every child in some way or other, whether it be welcoming a VIP, designing the cover of the handout, operating the slide projector or tape recorder, taking part in a dramatization of some feature of the work, or acting as presenter on a video-film made on equipment borrowed from the teachers' centre.

An exhibition or part of it often has the chance of a second life, e.g. at a teachers' centre, college of education, shopping centre, swimming baths entrance hall or the local pub or church. This will further delight the children and reinforce knowledge in this particular project area.

The Roles of the Teacher

Throughout this book suggestions have been made on how project work in the primary school might be approached. Such proposals require teachers to examine the various roles which they might play if the suggestions were to be adopted. Much will depend upon the individual teacher. The quality of classroom life which the teacher has successfully built up is a key factor. This will include the particular relationships which have been developed with the children as well as the teacher's particular approach(es) to the task of teaching.

A change of approach will, however, often require a change of role, and a change of attitude. The teacher must make the decisions about what will be allowed in the way of interaction between children, movement in class, degree of independence and choice. A more individual approach, where the emphasis is upon children thinking and doing for themselves, requires more from the teacher – and a variety of roles.

There will be times when the teacher is an *instructor,* particularly when new skills are required by the children; it may also apply when some facts are to be learnt although I would prefer the term *teacher* for this activity. In choosing progressive methods the educative role of the teacher will still be dominant – and there will be occasions when this will be narrowly defined. There was a period when someone 'caught' teaching didactically to a whole class was acutely embarrassed. All kinds of devices were adopted to prevent this happening – even moving the blackboard off centre, so that it could only be used to illustrate some aspect of learning to a small group. Colleges of education at the time may have assumed that this skill was no longer required, because graduating students would volunteer that they had never been told about class teaching.

The teacher will frequently act as a *discussion leader* when, before and after various educational experiences, there is the important business of a guided, structured exchange of ideas and impressions. So the rather orthodox role of a teacher needs to be modified from providing a daily dose of imparted facts to a two-way process of communication with individuals and groups of different sizes – and frequently the whole class.

Where facts and knowledge are available to the class through a system of resources (of which the teacher is one), it will be important to see that the information is not indigestible, incorrect or redundant. In considering the teacher as *a resource*, a number of points need to be kept in mind. A teacher who is interested in the subject will usually have some knowledge and understanding and can therefore directly assist the child. This does not mean providing a ready-made answer to every query; it means guiding children towards a solution in such a way that they are doing some if not most of the work. There will be occasions (possibly quite a few) when the teacher does not know. This is an opportunity for the teacher to suggest how a solution might be found, or to work and learn alongside the child – helping to find the answer, and even acting as a model of how to go about the process of finding out. However, the child will become disillusioned with both the subject and the teacher if the latter appears to know nothing about a particular topic. This raises the whole question of whether children ought to be allowed to embark upon a project about which the teacher is both ignorant and lacking in enthusiasm.

Enthusiasm in a teacher and interest in the subject will have an important bearing on the project's success. If the teacher feels no enthusiasm for the project, then it will probably seem very dull to the children. An element of surprise and novelty should get the project off to a good start, but it will be the communication of the teacher's own delight in what the class is doing which will give the work that necessary lift. So the teacher has to be a *stimulator* of the class as the children become involved in some aspect of learning about the real world. The skilful and experienced teacher will make shrewd choices of method to suit the child(ren), the particular objectives for that part of the project, the constraints of the situation (e.g. when the children are out of doors/in a museum/engaged in activities which might impinge upon others) or any other special circumstances (e.g. a flagging of interest at some point in the project), and will provide a degree of variety and balance in the programme. Flexibility is important and readiness to react to direct feedback, for example discovering that the work is too easy or too difficult, or that the enthusiasms of the class are carrying the project in a particular direction.

No class or individual child should be expected to give up on a mere whim or just because the going is a little tough. This is particularly important where the pupils have exercised a choice.

Much of the time, the teacher will function as *adviser or consultant*, using the language of discussion to inspire, encourage, prod, clarify and interpret, draw out, question, stimulate thought, guide and develop both the subject matter and the children. By adopting this role the teacher will be bringing out the range of possibilities in a situation, raising challenging questions in relation to the work, sustaining the children over a difficult patch, discussing potentially useful avenues to explore, drawing things out and bringing them together.

An early and continuing role will be that of *project planner*. This includes master-minding the study from its beginning as a 'twinkle in the eye' through all the processes of gestation, birth and subsequent development. The teacher will need also to be a *manager of resources*. Too often a project fails because it is inadequately resourced. This can sometimes apply to a local study where little information and illustration is available. The teacher needs to acquire significant and relevant materials for use during the project. These can be borrowed, bought or made, but the teacher will need to use professional judgement to balance the outlay of time and money to provide an adequate resource bank which need not be made available to the children all the time. Anticipation of needs will be an important feature, and experience and discussion with other teachers will help to plan carefully what is required.

The teacher must obviously be a *supervisor* who is there to ensure that children learn. This will include determining a code of conduct and a set of procedures all of which are designed to help the work run smoothly in an agreeable atmosphere. It will include checking on the work of individuals and groups, correcting errors, establishing points, ensuring that work is proceeding satisfactorily – that one child is not struggling or another coasting along. As much of this controlling activity as possible should be done with the child or the group and so in a sense the teacher might be seen in a *tutorial* role. It will be important to keep a record of children seen and some reference to the present 'state of play' of the project as a whole. Supervision is required however well motivated the children are. If a teacher does not appear to be interested in their work, children will be less inclined to bother. We all need others to take an interest in what we do and offer encouragement. Appreciation must not be indiscriminate, nor criticism destructive. Within the unstreamed classes, the more able child is often left to his own devices. Such a child may also be an underachiever, and need help in the same way as the average and the least able child does. Linked with this aspect will be the teacher as *evaluator* of the project, and each contribution to it, as well as of individual performance. Once again experience and judgement will come into this work of appraisal.

Where a number of teachers are cooperating, then a leader needs to take on the role of *coordinator* to ensure that everyone is involved; talents, interests and experiences are known; ideas pooled, resources shared, mutual support provided and opportunities given and taken to plan, discuss and develop the project. Responsibility for the major planning might rotate topic by topic, and term by term.

Evaluation

Today, and for some time to come, it is and will be important for the teacher to evaluate the work which is being done in class. It will be important for teachers not to be stampeded into spending so much time testing that they have little left for teaching, or to confine themselves to those aspects of the curriculum which can be readily tested, since those may not include the very areas we are discussing in this book.

The project needs to be evaluated because:

1   it represents a significant part of the term's or year's work;
2   the teacher will want to know which features require improvement;
3   the teacher will want to assess what each child has gained from the experience.

Informed professional judgement should figure highly in deciding which strategies to employ. Any experienced teacher who has carried out a number of projects will know whether the latest one has been as successful as those done in previous terms. In making this subjective judgement the teacher will consider a number of things:

1   the composition of the class and how it has varied from the school norm at that age-level, or from a similar group known from another school;
2   the particular project;
3   the way children bring in materials, talk about something related to the project that has been on television or in the newspaper;
4   the way that parents comment when they meet the teacher informally – 'You've got that boy of mine besotted with the Normans', 'His dad has been to the library himself to find out more about electric motors', 'Is it true you're wanting photographs from their grandparent's albums?'
5   the looks of the children's faces when it is announced that it is project time, or that a group can finish a particular piece of collective writing they are doing.

All these and·more will indicate the enjoyment and interest in the work in hand.

The individual books and work collections should be looked at regularly, preferably alongside the child, so that constructive comments can be made and advice given. By examining a piece of work the teacher will gain some idea of the knowledge and understanding of the pupil. A short discussion will confirm or modify this first assessment. The quantity and quality of work presented may indicate the level of interest and application. Comment can then be made in a record book and this compared with earlier statements and assessments. The difference between appraisals could be significant, either because there has been a deterioration or a dramatic improvement in interest, comprehension and work output.

Where the children are working in permanent groups, the teacher can make regular checks to make sure that all is going satisfactorily, that all in the team are pulling their weight, that the leadership is doing what it was intended to do, that progress towards a particular end is being made. It is important that there is equal opportunity for everyone to contribute in a variety of ways, and especially to avoid a situation in which some children simply do the menial tasks.

All of this work of assessment is very time-consuming and the teacher, preoccupied with the day-to-day running of the class as well as the conduct of the project, may be rather short of time for evaluation as well. Therefore it is important to be systematic about it, seeing individuals and groups in a particular order (or more often when more detailed checking is obviously necessary for a few in the class). Also it is useful for the teacher to note down any special happening during the day – a particular child's responses during an oral lesson, or on a fieldtrip – which can be written up at the end of the day.

There is nothing wrong with some old-fashioned questioning to find out the extent of the children's knowledge. This can be done in a short period at the end of the morning, or it can be a pencil and paper test with questions carefully thought out and not simply 'pulled out of the air'. The information gained should tell the teacher as much about class interest in the project as anything else, i.e. where the gaps in knowledge are and where a new approach or reinforcement would be beneficial. In classes where the children are grouped, each group could be given an assignment of writing a general knowledge quiz relating to the project.

It is valuable for the children to be encouraged to provide feedback on the project themselves, either in a discussion or on paper. It may come as something of a surprise to find out which features of the project the children found most interesting and which most boring. The children can also be asked to rank in order of merit ten identified aspects of the study and to say what things they found easy to do, and which difficult.

A teacher can always ask another colleague to come into the classroom to talk with the children, look both at work in progress and at completed work and offer an overall, critical view. Where there is trust and understanding the good points could be specified as well as the less-successful features. There is no reason why a teacher from another school should not make some informal comments about a project. It is of course important for the teacher to tell the head about the project and to find out what he or she thinks of the work which the class has carried out. The local adviser should be able to provide valuable objective comments.

Earlier in the book, the question of general aims and specific objectives was discussed. It will be essential, therefore, to look back at the particular objectives set for the project, to see how far the goals have been met. It may be that the objectives were not realistic; on the other hand it may be that individuals in the class simply failed to reach them for a variety of reasons. Where possible, tests should be devised to check on competence and understanding. The use of a compass, or map; the operation of a tape recorder or a clinometer; the making of a rubbing or a print can be quickly carried out, and assessment made of the degree of success achieved. Evaluation work of this nature can have an element of diagnosis built into it and the teacher can take appropriate remedial action to assist particular children.

Where a school record card does not incorporate a reference to project work (or environmental studies) then the teacher should add information relating to this work, including references to any special contribution a child has made to a joint venture.

With greater stability in staffing, and a greater concern about continuity in the primary school today, teachers should confer when transferring children between classes (and to secondary schools) and make particular reference to project work where it has been a significant part of the class work for the past year(s).

3 Approaches to Project Work

The answer to the question, 'How should one approach project work?' should be 'with enthusiasm, confidence (in oneself and the method of working) and a degree of variation'. All teachers have a style or range of styles to suit classroom circumstances. While some remain rooted firmly in one particular mode, others change – as they gain professional confidence; as different ideas are introduced through books, courses and colleagues; as classroom sizes go up or down; and with different age-groups. As teachers look for a different approach, or are encouraged to do so by internal or external pressures, it is valuable to examine the various options. The children themselves will appreciate modifications in their project work. The same diet day after day, however sound nutritionally, does pall after a while. Nor is it essential to search for a complete change on each occasion. Small and subtle changes can be quite sufficient for both the children and the 'cook'.

Approach A: General integrated
Projects selected in this group would be, by definition, those which could only be adequately studied within an undifferentiated curriculum. After an introduction to the theme, various aspects are studied through information, research, visits, discussions and formal lessons. The teacher may have to place some parameters around the project because of a time restraint, but the end product would indicate a thorough investigation of the topic. It will usually be helpful to divide up the project into its constituent parts for planning purposes.

Examples: The Street; Our Town; France; Food.

Approach B: Subject-orientated
This simply means that there is an identifiable subject bias to the choice of theme. Links with other disciplines can be brought in but it is likely that the main subject will dominate throughout. The special nature of the subject will often dictate certain features of this type of project, e.g. there is a likelihood that there would be more experiments in a science topic; more visits to museums and famous buildings in a history topic; more general fieldtrips in geographical studies. In schools where more formal work is the norm, this could be the approach adopted.

Examples:
Science Air, Fire, The Seashore, Autumn into Winter; Space.

History The Normans; Queen Elizabeth I; Nelson; Transport; How Our Grandparents Lived.
Geography Africa; The Story of Our Food; The River; The Polar Region.

Approach C: Serial story

Children enjoy a good story, and if this approach can be adopted and carried on for a number of weeks, there will be a keen sense of anticipation as project time is announced. This device may be particularly useful when timetable constraints make it impossible to carry out project work daily, and there is a need to have a strong linking thread.

Examples:

The River (The fact that this topic was suggested under Approach B confirms that there is no one exclusive way to deal with a project.) Each week work could focus upon a section of the river, e.g.

    Week 1 – The source
    Week 2 – The upper reaches
    Week 3 – The middle course
    Week 4 – The lower reaches
    Week 5 – The estuary.

Joseph and His Brothers
1   The family
2   The quarrel and selling of Joseph
3   Joseph in Egypt
4   Joseph in prison
5   The famine and reinstatement
6   The family reunited.

Further stories from RE – Pilgrim's Progress, The Journeys of Paul. A variety of tales could be used in this way from *Treasure Island* to *Watership Down*.

Approach D: Centre of interest

In this type of project, the starting point or nucleus can be quiet small, but by a series of moves through ever-widening circles the study can develop in all kinds of different ways. Sybil Marshall in *Adventure in Creative Education* (1968) described the way in which many weeks of stimulating work arose from her reading of Andrew Marvell's poem 'Upon Nun-Appleton House'. Taking inspiration from her example, I have used the poem 'Kilcash' by Frank O'Connor as a starting point for a project (see p. 107). Similarly a piece of music could be used or a photograph or a drawing or painting. Activities other than creative writing may well arise from such stimuli, and the teacher needs to be prepared for different developments. A coin, a shell, a stuffed bird, an old key or a bonnet are examples of objects which could be used as starters and lead towards a study of shops, the seashore, flight, etc.

Approach E: Symphonic

The emphasis here is on aesthetics and creativity. Every opportunity is taken to introduce music, art, craft, and drama to enable the children to experience each of these expressive forms as developed by different artists. As far as possible this would be first-hand experience at concerts and art galleries, but the child's imaginative world would also be enlarged through film, photographic reproductions, records and the printed word. From much of the stimuli there would be responses – discussion, and impressions in writing and drawing. In addition the children would be encouraged to make music themselves, perform in improvised drama periods, and create using various media and techniques, e.g. pottery, weaving, dyeing, photography.

Examples:
The Orchestra; The Arts; Beauty; Colour; The Shape of Things.

Approach F: Problem-centred

In this approach the teacher and the children are looking at some issue or event and trying to make sense of it by examining it closely. What will be thrown up will be a series of questions which might in their turn pose more queries but should by discussion, consideration of evidence, ideas and opinions, develop insights and understanding.

Eric Midwinter said that 'A child is an historical character in a geographical setting with moral and technical problems'. By adopting this approach and considering the local environment, we may be able to help the children to solve some of these problems.

Examples:
A Neighbourhood – an examination of the reasons for it being there, the changes it has undergone, what kind of people have lived and worked there in the past as well as now, why it is prospering or in decline, how it might be improved, and what must be done to make it better.
Clothes – why people wear what they do; clothing for different ethnic groups, religions, jobs, climates, sexes, ages; changes in dress over the ages; the design of clothes, choice of materials, colour, texture.

Approach G: Individual topic

This educational issue has generated much anger and anxiety. The difficulties arise for the pupil when the teacher is not able to provide the kind of assistance the child still requires. Where the teacher has provided or got agreement on the general title for the work of the class (e.g. *Europe,* with each child selecting a particular country; *Industry,* with a choice of products; *Transport,* with firm decisions on who will do aeroplanes and who will tackle land vehicles) then the teacher will be able to provide resources to meet most needs, and be attuned to the general requirements of the total study. Where there is a completely free choice, the teacher will have to face a variety of problems. Time is the major one, and linked with this is the teacher's ability to 'tune in' to each individual child's needs. The teacher will need to conduct a number of lessons/discussions with the pupils on how to choose a topic, deciding what the student wants to know, how to find it, what to do with the information which has been gathered, etc. Each child needs therefore to be asked to think through the chosen subject, prepare a framework and make suggestions on procedure. At this stage it will be necessary for each child to have a personal tutorial with the teacher, who will make suggestions on approach, resources and activities before work starts. This may well be through a series of questions and suggestions: 'Have you thought of . . .?', 'Why don't you discuss this with David, who has done some work on . . .?', 'If we ask Mr Smith at playtime, I think we'll find he can help with . . .', 'If we look up this in the *Treasure Chest for Teachers,* I think there is an address you will find worth having . . .', 'Look up the January issue of *Junior Education,* and see if there are some ideas you could use there . . . .'

It may be essential to ask for the project to be re-planned after this first chat to avoid later disappointment. Some children will require a lot of sustained help. There is no point in looking at a particularly poor specimen project plan, and in desperation say 'Right – carry on' knowing that it will produce little in its present form. In project work the teacher must keep a watching brief on the children's work and sustain enthusiasm.

Project Guidelines

These project guidelines have been presented in a number of ways. Some are given in some detail, so that teachers can either adopt the complete plan or select from the various options. Some are given in 'skeleton' form so that teachers can add their own flesh and clothing. The final group consists, in many cases, of starting points which can be developed in a variety of ways.

Elsewhere in this book, the importance of gathering appropriate resources has been emphasized. As resources spending is cut in schools, education and county libraries, so there will inevitably be fewer books and other materials to enrich and inform the children. The teacher will often have to rely on the materials the school already possesses and perhaps manufacture other resources for project use. I have had to include details of materials which the school may not be able to purchase (or borrow because loan services are similarly restricted) or which may now be out of print (it is worth checking existing school stock and the local library to see if they have copies of books which are now unobtainable). Also listed are details of commercial and other organizations which produce publicity material and other information about their products or services. Costs have escalated and some firms have now had to reduce their educational departments and others now feel obliged to make a small handling charge.

A complex index of all materials which are available in the school will be invaluable at the planning stage. Neighbouring schools might develop arrangements for sharing resources, or even for collaborating on joint projects.

The Shopping Centre

This is a project for all seasons, places, ages and tastes, and because the study area is close to the school, it will be a cheap one – an important consideration today.

For the *very youngest children,* visits to the shops can be linked with the purchase of ingredients for cooking or foodstuffs for the various pets kept in school. The teacher can arrange for small groups of children to be escorted by adults (aides and/or parents) all of whom can talk to the children about the shops, the things they sell and the people who work there. If the shopping 'rush hour' is avoided, the staff at the various shops will have more time to attend to the educational as well as the consumer needs of the children.

In school, setting up a number of shops in turn will provide an opportunity to introduce practical work in money, weighing and measuring, as well as oral work. The making of a large frieze, with their own shops painted in position, could be the beginning of map work.

Lower juniors could make a number of visits, particularly if they are near a large shopping complex. The variety of shops which exists will provide opportunities for larger surveys, and perhaps for small group or individual studies of different types of shop. Some classification work – leading to graphical representation – should follow (e.g. shops could be grouped into those which sell foodstuffs; chemist shops; radio and television agents; other service establishments like launderettes and hairdressers).

Often the local borough surveyor, estate agents, or teachers' centres, have large-scale maps which can be copied for survey work. Sometimes the maps are out of date and so the children can check for up-to-date accuracy before they devise some coding system to record information about the shops. This data can be used to make a large-scale plan of the centre, with some 3-D modelling as an additional possibility.

Further individual projects can then be set up to trace the goods to their point of origin: the fruit and vegetables to orchard and farm via docks, airport or road; sugar to the beet fields of Lincolnshire or plantations on the other side of the world; frozen meat to New Zealand; bread to the wheatfield with the farmer, miller and baker all involved in various important stages in the process. Clothing would provide a small group with yet another line of enquiry. If the children take photographs, make short tape recordings of sound effects and interviews with the different shopkeepers, collect labels from supplies and 'dummies' from the various establishments, as well as empties from home, this should enable a lot of extra resources to be available for a variety of uses in art, craft and written activities.

Top juniors and children from *middle schools* can pursue more sophisticated studies and consider issues such as:

Why is the shopping centre on that particular site?
What was there before?
Why is there a particular number and type of shops?
Why are particular shops in different places?
How many banks, post offices, restaurants and cafés are in the area?
What transport services are available to bring in the customers?
How can we find out whether people are satisfied with the range of shops in the area?
What types of shops are open at unsocial hours?
What kinds of goods and services are not available to people?
How far have they got to go to get them?
How many people use a selected group of shops over a specific period during a day?

Other approaches might be adopted, perhaps using another set of questions:

How have people obtained the goods and services they need throughout time? in different countries today?
What are the advantages of grouping shops together?
What are the differences between the corner shop and the supermarket?
Why are the same goods marked at different prices in the same kinds of shop?
Why do some shops have to close down?
Why are some shops part of great chains?
Why are so many shops self-service institutions?
Why do shops have sales?

Through the use of books, pictures, film and television it will be possible to complement the experience gained by the children on fieldwork exercises so that they build up a growing knowledge of commercial life, trading through market and shop, some understanding of profit and loss, the nation's prosperity – with local significance, the nature of advertising, and for the oldest pupils, information about consumers' rights.

Resources

Reference books

Coates, M. (1973) *Shops* (People at Work Series) Chambers

Dorner, J. (1973) *Markets and Fairs* (Eyewitness Series) Wayland

Farnworth, W. (1976), *Shops and Markets* (On Location Series) Bell and Hyman

Gillett, C. (1977) *Shopping and Money Matters* Blackie

Gregory, O. B. (1972) *Shops and Markets* (Look Around You Series) Pergamon Press

Gundrey, E. (1976) *You and Your Shopping* Evans

Harrison, M. (1978) *Markets and Shops* Macdonald

Hyde, M. (1971) *The Shopkeeper* Macmillan

Mountfield, A. (1976) *Shops and Shopping* (Eyewitness Series) Wayland

Purton, R. (1973) *Markets and Fairs* (Local Search Series) Routledge & Kegan Paul

Thompson, S. (1976) *Shops and Markets* (Fact Finders Series) Macmillan

White, P. (1971) *Shops and Markets* A. & C. Black

Useful addresses

A number of commercial firms have produced aids for use in class projects:

Heinz Service to Schools, Hayes Park, Hayes, Middlesex

P.R. Department, J. Sainsbury, Stamford House, Stamford Street, London SE1

P.R.O., Tesco House, Delamare Road, Cheshunt, Herts.

Press Office, F. W. Woolworth, 242 Marylebone Road, London NW1

Shopping Centre Survey Sheet

Name of shop on fascia board

Name of owner or owning company

Name of manager	Number of employees
Type of shop	Size of shop

Number of similar shops within walking distance

Main goods or services	Where the goods come from

Where appropriate, list work of different departments and employees

Drawing or photograph of shopfront	Plan showing location of shop

Date of original building	Show access to delivery areas
Date shop opened	Numbers of customers using shop
Previous occupants	Between .... and ....
Dates of shop improvements and developments	.... and ....
	.... and ....

The Local Park

All cities and towns, and many villages, have a park which will be within reach of a school. A whole range of projects can be developed either for the whole class, groups or individuals.

Any investigation work should be done with the agreement of the park-keeper, whose goodwill will be indispensable. With his agreement, it may be possible to remove specimens. Normally only natural material which has fallen to the ground can be salvaged.

Park studies

1 Plants – cultivated, wild, weeds. Identification.
2 Trees – planted, self-sown, indigenous, exotic. Identification.
3 Soils. Basic geology.
4 Bird life: residents, migrants, waterfowl, birds of prey. Aviary.
5 Wild animal life: foxes, badgers, rabbits, mice, squirrels.
6 Animals in captivity: ponies, deer, sheep.
7 Tropical garden, water garden; summer house; plant nursery.
8 Fungi, lichens, galls.

9   Lakes and ponds. Rivers and streams. Animal and plant life.
10   Map work, surveys, data collection. Nature trails.
11   Insect life: bees and wasps, butterflies and moths.
12   The park itself: size, facilities, keepers, gardeners, other workers, bye-laws, opening hours – winter/summer, survey of users at different times of the day.
13   Machinery and tools in use.
14   Play facilities: Sand pit, paddling pools, swings and roundabouts – applications of scientific principles in recreation area – boating pool, donkey rides.
15   Organized games facilities: football, cricket, athletics, bowls, putting.
16   Entertainment: band concerts, summer shows, travelling circus.
17   Weather studies: observation work. If the park has a Stevenson Screen data can be collected by arrangement with the superintendent.
18   Refreshment facilities in or near the park: kiosks, travelling vans, drinking fountains, toilet facilities.
19   Vandalism. Litter. Pollution.
20   The Park and history: previous land use, famous building or monument. Famous events – tree planting. Use of park during wars.

Activities which can be carried out by the children include photography, sketching, rubbings, plaster casting, measurement – distances, angular or linear, height finding of trees, girth and spread.

Further ideas from:

Williams, C. (1975) *What You Can Find in a Park*. A. & C. Black
Edlin, H. (1971) *The Public Park* (Local Search Series) Routledge & Kegan Paul
Jackman, L. (1976) *Exploring the Park* Evans
Purton, R. (1975) *Parks and Open Spaces* Blandford

There will be a need for a great many reference books, to identify trees, flowers, fungi, birds, insects, etc. Some of these, especially the smaller pocket type, can be taken back and forwards to the park while the main works can be kept in school.

This project can run throughout a school year, so that seasonal change, and its effect on the park-keepers' work, can be observed. Alternatively, the park can be used for field observations during a project on Winter, or Summer into Autumn.

The whole project can be art-based, with the children adopting a particular plant or animal and making a special study of it, including detailed work with brush, pen or pencil.

The Local Park: Activity Planning Sheet*

Activities Features	Observations	Collections	Art/craft	Maths/ science	Other activities
Trees					
Other plants					
Large animals					
Small animals					
Insects & mini-beasts					
Birds					
Water					
Recreational facilities					
Historical aspects					
Other features					

Code: I Individual; G Group; C Class

* This kind of activity planning sheet can be adapted to different situations.

The Church

This project could engage a whole class for a month; it could be part of the study of a country town, village or urban borough; it could provide a focus for RE work, which in turn might be looking at different religions and the ways in which people worship; it might be a local study which has a particular sense of urgency because the church is standing empty and is about to be demolished or sold.

Figure 10   The church – lines of enquiry

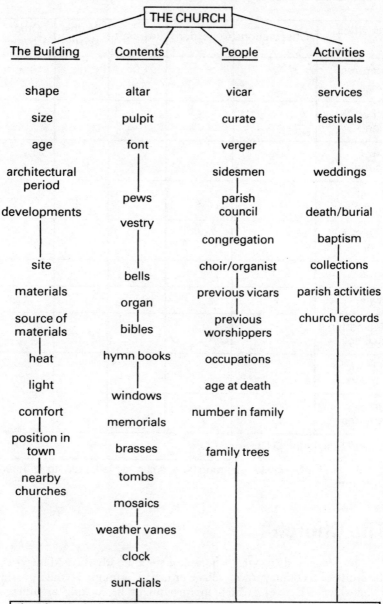

THE CHURCH			
The Building	Contents	People	Activities
shape	altar	vicar	services
size	pulpit	curate	festivals
age	font	verger	
architectural period		sidesmen	weddings
developments	pews	parish council	death/burial
	vestry	congregation	baptism
site		choir/organist	collections
materials	bells	previous vicars	parish activities
source of materials	organ	previous worshippers	church records
heat	bibles		
light	hymn books	occupations	
comfort	windows	age at death	
position in town	memorials	number in family	
nearby churches	brasses	family trees	
	tombs		
	mosaics		
	weather vanes		
	clock		
	sun-dials		

drawing; painting; rubbing; writing; composing – poems, stories, music; measuring; counting; interviewing; modelling; photography; researching.

An expert guide and enthusiast can transform a visit to a church. Some incumbents are well able to do this for adult visitors, but children are a different proposition. Perhaps the teacher can work with the vicar in showing the children around the building, pointing out particular aspects likely to interest them, allowing the children to handle things, and above all arranging various activities. A number of successful fieldtrips to a local church will produce plenty of stimulating follow-up work on return to class.

Various types of activity can be associated with the different facets of the church – both inside and out. Where the children's imagination is stimulated by one or more features, they should be encouraged to pursue those lines of enquiry on an individual basis and pool the results (see p. 72).

As indicated in the work plan, the lifespans of former parishioners can be discovered on the various memorials and gravestones. On one visit to a church in the Forest of Dean sharp-eyed children spotted the gravestone of John Reynolds, a keeper, who had died in May 1740, aged 47 years. Inside the church, there was a splendid memorial to Thomas Pyrke, a Justice of the Peace, a Deputy Lieutenant of the County, and a Deputy Constable of the Castle of St Breovall (now St Briavells). He had also been a Verderer of the Forest. He had died at the age of 65, on March 2nd 1752. The children felt it was reasonable to assume that these two must have known each other, in the roles of servant and master, and so efforts were made to re-create the kinds of conversations they might have had. Help from our hosts in Gloucestershire, who worked in present-day forests, ensured reasonably correct vernacular and content.

Another example of work triggered off by an interesting tombstone is a project based on the memorial in Woolwich, raised by public subscription, to the hundreds of dead who drowned following the sinking of the *Princess Alice* when it was in collision with a collier the *Bywell Castle* on 3rd September 1878. Nearby is the gravestone to Captain Grinstead of the ill-fated vessel, along with his wife and daughter who had been on the pleasure trip that day. The event in Woolwich Reach is well documented, and from this starting point a considerable project developed with drama, the study of leisure and costume in Victorian times, as well as safety on ships, being special features.

The Railway Station

'Transport' is such a wide area that the class and teacher can be defeated by its very size. However, a subdivision of the subject can provide the opportunity for some study in depth. Where a school has chosen 'Transport', then each class could opt for an aspect of the subject.

In spite of the closing of many branchlines, there is still a network of railways which covers the country. Most schools – especially those in urban areas – would be within reach of a working railway station. Some would also be near a mainline station or even a terminus, both of which provide opportunities for activities.

Safety would be a special concern for the teacher on such an excursion, and extra adult supervision should be arranged. Permission to visit should be requested from the station-manager, and his cooperation enlisted to make the trip a successful one.

In different parts of the country enterprising groups have re-established short sections of railway line. Such groups have tried to preserve steam trains, and the various contemporary features like rolling stock and platform furniture, so a visit to a nearby railway trust or company will be a journey into the past. A trip on a steam train, and time to examine the museum exhibits which are often a feature of such enterprises, will provide facts and impressions which can be stored and used later. Examples of these societies are: North Yorkshire Moors Railway, Keighley and Worth Valley Railway (used in the film of *The Railway Children*), Bluebell Railway, Severn Valley Railway and Festiniog Railway.

Visits to certain museums and collections will also enable the children to see examples of every aspect of railway evolution, e.g. The Railway Museum at York, the Science Museum in London, The Stockton and Darlington Museum and The Open Air Museum at Beamish in County Durham (where there is a railway station, signal box and the chance to make a short journey on a train).

The booklets *Museums and Galleries* (Index Publications) and *Historical Transport Guide* (Transport Trust, 18 Ramillies Place, London W1V 2BA) are invaluable sources of information for this and many other projects.

If the teacher is not a frustrated model-engine enthusiast, there are likely to be some pupils (and parents) in the class who are. What finer way to learn about railway procedure than to have a model railway layout? Cooperation between owners of stock could produce a complex system. Craft work within this project could well include making landscape models to use with such a layout. There are model railway societies in many areas and the secretary could be approached for practical help.

British Transport Films, Melbury House, Melbury Terrace, London NW1 have a number of well-produced films in their catalogue. *Night Mail* and *Snow* are two titles which spring to mind, firstly because they are so successful with children of all ages, and secondly because of unusual features in the films themselves. (*Night Mail* uses W. H. Auden's poem of the same name, and music by Benjamin Britten. *Snow* has no dialogue or commentary of any kind.)

Honneger's suite *Pacific 231* is another powerful piece of music which could be used to stimulate music-making from the children. Older juniors and middle-school pupils will enjoy the story of a brave engine driver who stuck to his controls to prevent a serious accident. The tale is dramatically told in one of the sadly-missed radio ballads, *Driver Axon* (Argo Records RG 474).

The centenary of another great railway calamity has just passed. The event is remembered in 'The Tay Bridge Disaster' by William McGonegal. Other useful poems are:

de la Mare, Walter 'The Railway Junction'
Eliot, T. S. 'Skimbleshanks, The Railway Cat'
Hardy, Thomas 'Midnight on the Great Western'
Pudney, John 'Valediction for a Branch Railway'
Spender, Stephen 'The Express'
Stevenson, R. L. 'From a Railway Carriage'

The children may enjoy songs like 'Casey Jones', 'Cosher Bailey', and the 'Gospel Train'.

The emphasis in this project has been on experience, either direct or through poets and music makers. Project work should not be exclusively concerned with data-collection; it is just as important for the children to form impressions with the help of those who have looked and listened before; and to compare what they have seen with what others have also experienced. Of course all kinds of I-Spy tasks, interviews with porters, ticket-collectors, left-luggage attendants, kiosk assistants, etc., timetable study, art work, etc. will take place. Such activities also have their place and the material can be used for written work – fact or fiction – which in its turn could become part of the children's own railway radio ballad.

The Layers of a Town

The secret of success is sometimes no more than looking at something familiar in a different way. This project relies on a new perspective. Instead of studying a town or an area in two dimensions, the children are introduced to almost the same subject, with the vertical plane added. Studying the layers of a town is rather like being by turns an underground worker, a pedestrian, a passenger on the top deck of a double-decker bus, the driver of a huge crane, and finally a helicopter pilot.

The whole class may prefer to consider all aspects of the project, or to opt for one particular level and study all the features associated with it,

Figure 11 The layers of a town – ideas and linking themes

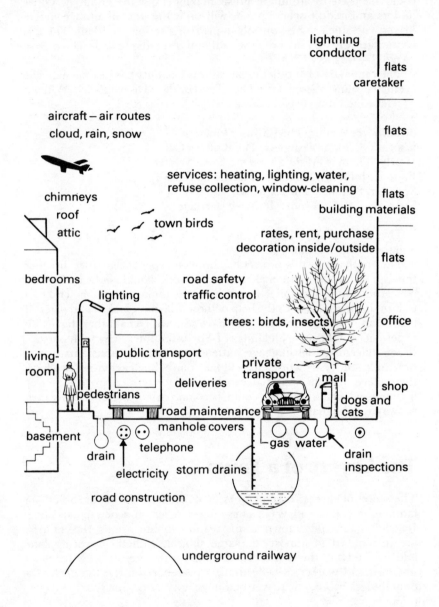

lightning conductor

flats

caretaker

aircraft – air routes

cloud, rain, snow

flats

services: heating, lighting, water, refuse collection, window-cleaning

chimneys

roof

attic

town birds

flats

building materials

rates, rent, purchase

decoration inside/outside

flats

bedrooms

road safety

traffic control

lighting

trees: birds, insects

office

public transport

living-room

private transport

mail

deliveries

shop

pedestrians

dogs and cats

road maintenance

basement

manhole covers

gas water

drain

telephone

electricity

storm drains

drain inspections

road construction

underground railway

and then set about finding interesting ways of telling the others about those things happening in their study layer. All kinds of art work are possible – a vertical frieze would certainly be different. There are dramatic possibilities as characters from different 'floors' get to know each other.

Alongside a 'slice' of the townscape, some early ideas and linking themes are suggested on p. 76.

It would not require too great a leap of the imagination to translate this concept of the vertical layers into the natural world. The emphasis would then be upon plants and animals, with some links with people. But as one pursued *Project Oak Tree* or *Project Forest,* what would emerge as surely as it does if looking at a town or city, is the interdependence of the different parts of the system.

Food

Many urban schools, particularly in the larger conurbations of London, Birmingham, Liverpool, etc., have a multi-ethnic group of children. Schools which do not have such diverse groups within their schools, nevertheless do exist in a multi-cultural society and should acknowledge this through their curriculum.

There are topics which can be quite deliberately chosen because they span the interests, experiences and common needs of all children. Homes, Clothes, Work, Customs all come within this category. Food has been taken as a particular example of such a project. Not only does it happen to be an interesting subject in its own right – with some very enjoyable practical activities involved – but it also impinges very much upon health education, to which increasing attention is given in schools today (as well as through the present campaign directed at the adult population). Another facet of a project on food is the way in which parents can assist both inside and outside the school. Food can feature as an aspect of geographical and historical studies, as well as animal and plant projects.

Resources
Two very useful planning books for this project are:

Food, A Resource For Learning in the Primary School ILEA Learning
  Materials Service, Highbury Station Road, London N1 and
Waters, D. *Learning About Food* National Dairy Council

Books
Baker, M. (1975) *Food and Cooking* Black
Ferguson, S. (1971) *Food* Batsford (she has also written the parallel book *Drink*)
Hay, D. (1976) *Things in the Kitchen* Collins
Kincaid, D. and Coles, P. (1977) *Food* Hulton Educational (emphasizes science aspect)
Sedgewick, U. (1969) *My Learn to Cook Book* Hamlyn
Swayne, D. (1978) *I am a Chef* Dent

Useful addresses
Many of the institutions and firms listed issue free or cheap teachers' and pupils' materials. It is a good idea to keep the list up to date through advertisements, or comment in the educational press, and add any new details sent through the post.

Apple and Pear Development Council, Union House, The Pantiles, Tunbridge Wells, Kent

Association of Agriculture, Victoria Chambers, 16–20 Strutton Ground, London SW1P 2HP

British Egg Information Service, 37 Panton Street, London SW1X 4EW

British Farm Produce Council, Agriculture House, London SW1 7NJ

British Gas, Room 414, 326 High Holborn, London WC1V 7PT

British Meat Service, Meat and Livestock Company, PO Box 44, Queensway House, Bletchley, Milton Keynes MK2 2EK

British Sugar Beet Company, 140 Park Lane, London W1

Brooke Bond Oxo, Education Service, Leon House, High Street, Croydon

Butter Information Council, The Pantiles House, 2 Neville Street, Tunbridge Wells, Kent

Canned Foods Advisory Service, Education Department, 39 Charing Cross Road, London WC2

Central Electricity Generating Board, Publicity Department, Sudbury House, 15 Newgate Street, London EC1 7AU

Cheese from Switzerland, 1 Amersham Hill, High Wycombe, Bucks.

Christian Aid, PO Box 1, London SW9 8BH

Christian Education Movement, 2 Chester Houses, Pages Lane, London N10 1PR

Dairy Produce Advisory Service, Milk Marketing Board, Thames Ditton, Surrey KT7 0EL

Danish Agricultural Products, 2–3 Conduit Street, London W1

Eggs Authority, Union House, Eridge Road, Tunbridge Wells, Kent

Eden Vale, Rossmore Road, London NW10

Flour Advisory Bureau, 21 Arlington Street, London SW1A 1RN

General Dental Council, 37 Wimpole Street, London W1M 8DQ
Gibbs Oral Hygiene Service, Hesketh House, Portman Square, London W1A 1DY
Health Education Council, 78 New Oxford Street, London WC1A 1AH
Heinz Service for Schools, Hayes Park, Hayes, Middlesex MXUB 8AL
Kellogg Company of Great Britain, Public Affairs, Stretford, Manchester M32 8RA
Lyons-Tetley United, Consumer Relations Department, 325 Oldfield Lane, Greenford, Middlesex
Mattessons Meats, c/o Aquarious Griswold PR, 39 Victoria Street, London SW1
Ministry of Agriculture, Fisheries and Food, Tolcarne Drive, Pinner, Middlesex HA5 2DT
Mothercare Limited, Cherry Tree Road, Watford, Herts
National Dairy Council, John Princes Street, London W1M 0AP
National Farmers Union, Agriculture House, London SW1X 7NJ
Oxfam, Educational Department, 274 Banbury Road, Oxford OX2 7DZ
Potato Marketing Board, 50 Hans Crescent, London SW1X 0NB
Rank McDougall Hovis Foods Limited, RHM Centre, PO Box 551, 152 Grosvenor Road, London SW1
Royal Society for the Prevention of Accidents, Cannon House, The Priory, Queensway, Birmingham B4 6BS (accidents in the kitchen)
The Tea Council, Sir John Lyon House, 5 High Timber Street, Upper Thames Street, London EC4V 3NJ
Understanding Electricity, The Electricity Council, 30 Millbank, London SW1P 4RD
White Fish Authority, 10 Young Street, Edinburgh EH2 4JQ

Activities
Visits to: shops, farms, market gardens, food manufacturing factories; museums – to study food and cooking in earlier times; exhibitions featuring food, e.g. agricultural shows often feature cake-making competitions, etc., and particular firms may give demonstrations.

People and firms may come into the school to give a talk or demonstration, show films, etc. We invited the local baker to come in and judge the children's efforts at breadmaking. We were also able to arrange to have a milking cow stay in the school grounds for a week. Children attended the twice daily milking sessions, and helped to clean out the animal and her sleeping quarters.

During a school European project, the cook was able to cooperate (in slightly happier economic times than these) and produce a different menu each day, linked with one of the countries being studied. There was a daily queue simply to see the menu, and then later in the day to enjoy its special taste. The children will want to cook themselves and

Figure 12   Food

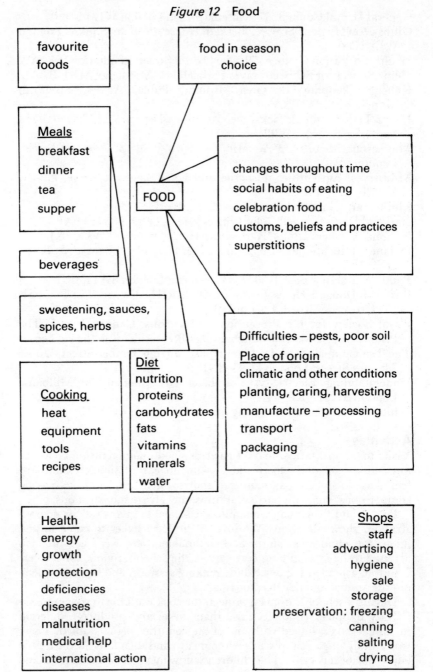

the business of selecting suitable recipes, purchasing the materials, weighing the ingredients, mixing and preparing for the oven (where appropriate) and timing the process, will be as exciting as eating the finished product. Local authorities and schools will have safety procedures which must be adhered to; the staff may have to become involved in a training programme for each other, ancillary workers and parents who might be engaged in cooking activities.

Foods from different countries can be prepared and eaten. Finding out how these foods are grown, cooked and served in the country of origin could be a project for small groups of children. Packets, labels, advertising matter of different kinds can be collected into folders, or made into wall charts.

Unusual beliefs, sayings, proverbs connected with food can be gathered as well as stories and rhymes. History books should reveal the diets of the peasant and king, the sailor and the monk. Parents and certainly grandparents will be able to tell the children about war-time diets when imports of food were very restricted (and people were much healthier!).

Picture-making could include scenes from the food-producing parts of the world; life-size models of fruit and vegetables would involve the children in craft work. These, alongside other written and art work the children had produced, would make a colourful display of sights, sounds, smells and tastes.

Wool

Wool has been chosen as a centre of interest because it has a long and interesting history, with lots of possibilities for project activities.

I recall visiting a sheep farmer in Herefordshire, when preparing a project on wool. I wanted some slides of the shepherd's work round the year, including the role of the sheep dog. The shepherd showed me the various things he did – even those out of season. Fortunately it was spring, and so there were lambs about. He needed to persuade a ewe that an orphan lamb could replace her own dead young one. This was done in front of the camera and tape recorder. I had my first visual and aural aids for the project, but before we parted company we – which included the shepherd's wife – sang *The Lord's My Shepherd* around a rather out-of-tune piano. It seemed the most natural thing in the world to do – and acted as a reminder at the planning stage to share with the class the stories about shepherds and sheep in the Bible.

The children in the class were later to visit a farm in North Wales where they saw the kinds of things I had been shown earlier, including this time sheep shearing and wool baling. The shepherd farmer was invited back to our temporary Welsh base and after dinner that night, with his dog at his feet, he talked for almost two hours with the children telling them about his life, the difficulties of working a mountain range, bad weather conditions and so on. Much of this was in response to the children's questions which were stimulated by their own enthusiasm, built up during the period of preparation, and the experiences earlier in the day.

We reached bedtime just as we had got onto the topic of losing of sheep as a result of diseases (a lot of them as it turned out). The shepherd was asked whether he had ever felt like giving up. He replied, 'No, you've got to have faith.' The final question came, 'What's it like caring for sheep?' The response was, 'It's a hard life, but I wouldn't change it for anything.' We turned those words into a chorus for a radio ballad tape in which the interviews, the sound effects, the stories and poems were brought together to make a story. Also included in the story was the visit to a dyeing and weaving mill, which proved to be a colourful and noisy experience.

Another class studying sheep used this tape with slides as part of their learning resources. They visited the Smithfield Show in December, where a special sheep demonstration had been arranged for children. At each of the major festivals, we tried to provide a new perspective. That Christmas, the celebration was entitled 'The Song of the Shepherd'. Not only were traditional carols sung, including those with obvious links, but also included were songs and poems which spoke of the shepherd and his flock.

Resources

Reference books
Cavanna, B. and Harrison, G. (1972) *Wool* Watts
Duncan, M. (1973) *Creative Crafts with Wool and Flax* Bell
Gagg, J. C. *Farms and Farming* Blackwell
Oxford Junior Encyclopedia – Vol. 6: Farming and Fisheries OUP
Stratford, A. (1972) *Introducing Knitting* Batsford
Sutton, A. *The Craft of the Weaver* BBC Publications
Watson, T. and J. *Wool for Warmth* Wayland
Whitlock, R. *Sheep* Wayland

Fiction
Gifford, G. *Jenny and the Sheep Thieves* Gollancz
Williams, S. *Lambing at Sheepfold Farm* Gollancz

Poems
Blake, William 'The Lamb'
Clare, John 'Sheep in Winter' and 'Shepherds Five'

Davies, W. H. 'Sheep'
Farjeon, Eleanor 'The Old Shepherds'
Hardy, Thomas 'A Sheep Fair'
Lewis, C. Day 'Sheepdog Trials in Hyde Park'
Pitter, Ruth 'Herding Lambs'
Ponchon, Steven 'Shepherd's Tale'
Young, A. 'The Shepherd's Hut'

Music

The Handloom and the Powerloom folk song
Mak, The Shepherd music by Herbert Chappell, libretto by Don Taylor, universal edition
Psalm 23
Searching for Lambs folk song
Shepherd Boy's Song (EMI CSD 3640)
The Shepherd's Calendar cantata for children by Peter Maxwell Davis
Shepherd's Hey Percy Grainger
Shepherd's Jig English Folk Dance Society (ED 102)
Shepherd's Song Willie Scott (Topic 12T 183)
We Shepherds Are The Best of Men (Topic 12T 150)
The Work of the Weavers folk song

Records

Cotswold Craftsmen Saydic SDL 247 (Track 1 Cotswold Sheep)

Films

English Wealth from Wool Central Office of Information, Central Film Library, Government Buildings, Bromyard Avenue, London W3 (Although quite old, this is a useful film about making yarn and weaving cloth.)
Export Lamb Education Department, Western Australia. Available in UK from Educational Media International (Australia), 25 Boileau Road, London W5
Sheep Ranch Country Education Department, United World Films, South-East Australia. Available in UK from Educational Media International (Australia), 25 Boileau Road, London W5
Weave Me A Rainbow Scottish Film Library, C.O.I.
The Wonder of Wool British Wool Marketing Board
The German Sheepdog Educational Foundation for Visual Aids

Journals

Farmer's Weekly, Farmer and Stockbreeder

Kits

British Wool E. J. Arnold and Son Ltd

Useful addresses

Association of Agriculture, Victoria Chambers, 16–20 Strutton Ground, London SW1P 2HP

British Wool Marketing Board, Education Department, Oak Mills Station Road, Clayton, Bradford, West Yorks BD1 6JD

The Guild of Weavers, Spinners and Dyers, c/o Miss R. Barne, 7 Railston Street, London SW3.

International Wool Secretariat, 6 Carlton Gardens, London SW1

National Farmers Union, Agriculture House, London SW1

Visits

Excursion to a sheep farm, if possible more than one to see different activities – lambing, shearing, dipping, the work of the sheep dog.

Sheep-dog trials and/or an agricultural show.

Agricultural college.

Sale of sheep at a country-town market.

Spinning and weaving factory, adult education institute where these crafts are practised.

Secondary school where there is a Rural Studies Department.

Museum to see exhibits relating to sheep farm and/or the woollen trade.

Classroom activities

Finding out about the woollen business and its contribution to England's history and economy; its effect upon localities, e.g. East Anglia with its great churches built from the wealth which came from wool; the Woolsack in Parliament; the work of the great inventors who changed weaving methods, e.g. Arkwright; sheep farming abroad – Australia and New Zealand, new trade routes – links with *Cutty Sark, The Witch of the Wool Run*.

Research into the life of the shepherd – use the writings of W. H. Hudson and Richard Jefferies, or Bob Copper whose first book *A Song For Every Season* (Methuen) tells of life as a shepherd half a century ago.

Learn about the wool trade through stories. Cynthia Harnett's story *The Woolpack* (Methuen) is an exciting adventure which can be serialized for the class.

Written work of various kinds can be stimulated by experiences inside and outside the school.

On visits to a sheep farm, or the countryside where sheep graze, it should be possible to collect wool from the hedgerow; with appropriate instructions and tools (see Dryads of Leicester catalogue, or the LEA supplies catalogue) it should be possible to learn how to card and spin wool, dye it, and weave it. Modest experiments can be conducted using simple card looms, before trying wooden looms with shuttles and heddles.

A study of the different sheep breeds could include a series of drawings; films could prompt the class to develop pictures showing scenes from an Australian or New Zealand sheep farm; reading extracts from Thomas Hardy's *Far From The Madding Crowd* might act as a stimulus for pictures showing the life of a shepherd in the last century. Three-dimensional models of the farmer and his flock could be used to create a calendar of the shepherd's year.

Canals

'Canals' fulfil many of the criteria for a potentially successful project: they are a piece of living history; they are colourful; you can go on them; there are plenty of resources to make research relatively easy: *Junior Education, Child Education* and *Art and Craft in Education* regularly feature the subject with plentiful illustrations (if the school has been circumspect, it will have back numbers readily available for use), and there are official and voluntary bodies who are anxious to promote interest and support for inland waterways.

While the golden era of canal building and use lasted from the second half of the eighteenth century for just less than 100 years, modern-day leisure use, as well as reduced commercial use, should be studied. Canals abroad, especially where there have been political, military and economic repercussions, should also be investigated, e.g. Suez and Panama.

Resources

Reference books
Aikman, R. *The Story of Our Inland Waterways* Pitman Publishing
Banks, J. *Fun on the Waterways* Penwork
Edwards, L. A. (1972) *Waterways of Great Britain* Imray
Farnworth, W. (1977) *Canals* Bell and Hyman
Hadfield, C. *British Canals* David and Charles
Hutchings, C. (1975) *The Story of Our Canals* Ladybird Books
McKnight, H. (1977) *The Shell Book of Inland Waterways* David and Charles
Parker, T. H. and Teskey, F. J. (1971) *Inland Waterways* Blackie
Pick, C. (1977) *Canals and Waterways* Macdonald Educational
Pierce, A. (1978) *Canal People* Black
Platt, J. (1981) *Canals* Macmillan Educational
Purton, R. (1972) *Rivers and Canals* Routledge and Kegan Paul
Ransom, P. (1977) *Your Book of Canals* Faber
Rice, P. (1976) *Narrow Boats* Dinosaur Press

Rolt, L. T. C. (1978) *Narrow Boats* Eyre and Spottiswoode
Ross, A. *Canals in Britain* Blackwell
Thornhill, P. (1959) *Inland Waterways* Methuen Educational
Vialls, C. (1976) *Canals* Black
Vince, J. *River and Canal Transport* Blandford
Whitlock, R. (1976) *Exploring Rivers, Lakes and Canals* E.P. Publishing
Wynyard, J. *Dams and Canals* Wheaton

Fiction
Carpenter, H. *The Joshers* Allen & Unwin
DeJong, M. *Far Out on the Long Canal* Lutterworth
Durward, M. *A Trip on the Canal* Nelson
Durward, M. *By The Canal* Nelson
Forester, C. S. *Hornblower and the Atropos* Michael Joseph (Chapter I –
   for the journey through Blisworth Tunnel)
Grahame, K. *The Wind in the Willows* Methuen (Chapter 10)
Krasilovsky, P. and Spier, P. *The Cow who fell in the Canal* World's Work
Wain, J. *Lizzie's Floating Shop* Bodley Head
Walsh, J. Paton *The Butty Boy* Macmillan

Charts
Building Britain's Canals British Waterways Board
Inland Waterways National Savings Poster

Kit
Waterways E.P. Publishing

Records
The English Canals Broadside Records
Narrow Boats BBC Record REB 56M and Argo ZTR 142
Straight from the Tunnel's Mouth by The Boatmen S.F.A. Recordings.
(The English Folk Dance and Song Society, 2 Regents Park Road,
   London W1, keep a library of canal folk songs.)

Filmstrips
London to Birmingham by Canal Common Ground
Panama Canal E.P. Publishing
The Panama Canal Unicorn Head
Suez Canal British Film Institute

Films
Afloat in Britain
The Gentle Highway
There Go The Boats   All obtainable from the
Waterways Our Heritage   British Waterways Board.
The World of Waterways

Canal Locks Gateway Films
The Jason British Film Institute
Narrow Boats British Film Institute

Useful addresses

Association of Waterways Cruising Clubs, 38 Sandhurst Drive, Ilford, Essex

British Waterways Board, Melbury House, London NW1 6JX

Canal Shop, Chewter Road, Nantwich, Cheshire

Canal Shop and Information Centre, 2 Kingston Row, Birmingham

Central Council for Physical Recreation, 70 Brompton Road, London SW3 (for water sports code)

Educational Use of Inland Waterways, National School Sailing Association, c/o Educational Cruises, Bottom Road, Four Marks, Lymington, Hants

Inland Waterways Association, 114 Regents Park Road, London NW1 8UQ

ROSPA, Royal Oak Centre, Brighton Road, Purley, Surrey C2R 2UL (for leaflet WS 44, *The Water Safety Rules*)

Waterways Educational Holidays, 115 Silbury Road, Warlingham, Surrey

Museums

Black Country Museum, Dudley, West Midlands
Bristol City Museum
Canal Exhibition Centre, Llangollen, Powys
City of Liverpool Museum
Cusworth Hall Museum, Doncaster, has a canal room
N.W. Museum of Inland Navigation, Ellesmere Port, Cheshire
Science Museum, Exhibition Road, London SW1
Waterways Museum, Stoke Bruerne, Northamptonshire

Canal trails

The British Waterways Board issues a leaflet on the current trails in use, and will give further details. Almost twenty are listed at the moment ranging from Westminster–Regent's Canal Dock in London, the Kennet and Avon at Bathampton, and the Shropshire Union Canal to the Stratford on Avon Canal. In addition there are some important canal features which can be seen if the school is close enough to visit, e.g. the Anderton Lift, Trent and Mersey Canal; 29 beam-locks at Devizes, Wiltshire; a flight of locks at Fort Augustus on the Caledonian Canal.

Theatre

The Magic Lantern Narrow Boat Theatre, 74 Rosebery Avenue, London EC1 run seasons of plays on narrow boats.

Canal trips

The highlight of the project could be a journey on a canal boat. These can be quite modest journeys or longer cruises which last several days. The question of safety and insurance will arise for any such ventures.

Adventure Cruises, Union Canal Carriers Ltd, 214 Whittington Road, London N22 (boat hire for longer cruises)

Grandwestern Horseboat Company, 15/16 West Mills, Newbury, Berks

Halcyon Cruises, Dept. 3, Canal Wharf, Oxford

Jason and butty boat Serpens: Little Venice to Camden (apply to Jason, Little Venice, London W2)

Jenny Wren trips: Camden Lock–Paddington (apply Camden Lock, Commercial Place, Chalk Farm Road, London NW1)

Linda Cruises (apply Mr and Mrs Crossley, Cosgrove Lock, Wolverton, Bucks)

School Journey Association of London, 43 Cavendish Road, London SW12 (enquiries about a five-day journey by narrow boat – Braunston to Rugby and return)

Activities

Study of the building of canals: when, how, where, why, by whom?

Study of the pioneers – Brindley, Telford, etc.

Consider the changes which took place during the main period of building.

The modern day use of canals for recreation.

The plant, animal and human life and activities linked with canals.

Stories and poems inspired by the experiences of the project.

Painting the traditional patterns, decorations and architecture.

Prepare OHP slides to show how a lock works.

Build a model lock.

Develop a canal system around the classroom, using window-sills and ledges.

Make a large-scale model of a narrow boat.

Create an interior scene from a narrow boat.

The Sea

The sea is the subject of legend, story, poem and songs; most countries, particularly our own, have a coastline of infinite variety and across it have moved invaders and explorers. A rich and varied animal and plant life is associated with it, particularly where the sea meets the land. Different approaches can be adopted which will make the project last a term, or half a term.

1   *A particular stretch of the coastline*
This theme would be appropriate for a school in a seaside town, or a class staying in one for an extended period. Instead of travelling all over the area visiting all the tourist attractions, the class activities for the week or fortnight's stay would be concentrated on the local area.

2   *General study of the coast*
Choose different kinds of coastline, e.g. sandy shore, estuary, salt marsh, rock pools, cliffs. At least one visit should be included in this project, but it could precede or follow the summer holidays, when many children would have visited the coast with their families.

3   *Study matrix*
This can be used to develop an intensive study of plant and animal life associated with the sea.

Figure 13   Study matrix

	Plants	Birds	Fish	Crustaceans
Beside the sea				
On the sea				
Above the sea				
Under the sea				

4   *A seaport*
Study could include import and export of goods and, with older children, be linked with our industrial history. The use of the port by passengers, especially those using car ferries (which some of the children will have experienced) is another aspect of the project. The particular kinds of work associated with the seaport are interesting, e.g. ship builders, customs and excise, ships' chandlers and seamen.

5   *A fishing port*
This could be linked with a particular port, e.g. Lowestoft, or another within easy reach of the school. The changing history of fishing; the trades linked with making fishing-nets, lobster-pot manufacture, kipper smoking. 'Life on a fishing boat', 'The big catch', 'A terrible journey', 'The loss of the . . . trawler' (each fishing port will have its tragedies, with local archives available for consultation).

6   *A mathematical and scientific approach to the sea*
Sea and River is the title of a Mathematics for the Majority, Continuation Project from the Schools Council. Although intended for secondary

children, the kit of work envelopes with extensive teaching notes would be fascinating for a lively interested group of fourth-year juniors, or children in the upper middle-school age-range. It is essentially a practical approach, with lots of materials to cut out and use as the children learn simple navigation, how to take bearings, find out how the moon causes tidal changes, what to pack into a container ship, forms of signalling at sea.

7   Famous sailors and explorers
There are many stirring tales of men from different countries who explored the oceans of the world and brought back both treasure and knowledge. One approach might be to introduce and illustrate each sailor in turn, and then extend the responsibility for follow-up activity to groups within the class. Here are suggestions for a first list: Prince Henry the Navigator, Christopher Columbus, Sir Francis Drake, Sir Walter Raleigh, Captain James Cook, Lord Nelson, Thor Heyerdahl.

8   Safety at sea
Regulations, Plimsoll lines, 'Rules of the Road', signalling flags and other communication methods. The work of the pilot, navigational techniques, maps and charts, bearings and soundings, shipwrecks, sinkings. The Coastguard Service, lifeboats, lighthouses, lightships and buoys.

The *Cutty Sark*

> They mark our passage as a race of men
> Earth will not look upon such ships as those again.
>   'Ships' John Masefield

Many schools in London and the home counties (and further afield) chose to visit Greenwich. The *Cutty Sark* usually provides the focal point for the day's planned activities. Other ships could readily be studied, using the following ideas as guidelines, e.g. *Gipsy Moth* (close by the *Cutty Sark*): the *Reliant*, inside the Maritime Museum at Greenwich; SS *Great Britain* at Bristol. A number of historic ships are moored at various Maritime Trusts, e.g. St Katherine's Dock, London (which includes the *Discovery*) and Exeter; HMS *Victory* at Portsmouth. From time to time, sailing ships gather in a port for a special event; very occasionally, for example when a special anniversary is imminent, a reproduction boat is built – a few years ago it was the *Golden Hinde*.

Resources

The *Cutty Sark* itself. In addition to the opportunities on the upper deck, between decks, and hold, the story of the ship is well told through pictures, text, models, a variety of other exhibits and recorded commentaries. The souvenir shop has a number of resources useful for preparatory and follow-up work, including rigging and sail charts, model kits of the *Cutty Sark* and other ships, and a number of reasonably priced, well-illustrated books and booklets.

Books

Carr, F. G. G. (1969) *'Cutty Sark'* Pitkin Pictorial
Hume, C. (1976) *'Cutty Sark': Last of the Racing Clippers* Modelbooks
Lubbock, B. *The Log of the 'Cutty Sark'* Brown, Son and Ferguson
Newton, D. and Smith, D. *The 'Cutty Sark'* Oliver and Boyd

Many books are available on the sea, and the age of the sailing ship is featured in many of them; selected examples could be included in the reference library.

Activities

In autumn 1970, the BBC took a particular event – an actual mutiny on the *Cutty Sark* – and created a music workshop from it. While the broadcast may not be available now, some schools may have kept the pupils' pamphlets which would present the opportunity to re-create the operetta.

Another well-documented part of history was the race between the *Cutty Sark* and the *Thermopylae*; this too could be brought to life in writing, music and drama.

The different owners and captains of the ship – Willis, Moodie and Woodget – can all be studied, as can the effect they had upon the various crews and voyages. This would link up with what life on board was like for the different crew members – the deckhands, cook, etc. – who had storms, poor food rations, hard task-masters, etc., to contend with.

Wool and tea were the main cargoes carried by the *Cutty Sark* and similar ships, and groups of children could study the growth, collection, manufacture and distribution of each of the products as well as their transportation by sea.

1 A film show

Sailing to the Cape (made in 1952 by G.B.I.) is a black and white film which provides dramatic pictures of the sea in all its moods, and particularly a heavy storm in the Roaring Forties.

2 *A poetry anthology*

The sea has appealed to many poets and so it is a simple matter to build up an anthology, which can be read by the children individually, or by the teacher to the class, or by volunteers. This particular arrangement was designed to give the impression of a complete voyage.

1   'Sea Fever' John Masefield
2   'A Wanderer's Song' John Masefield
3   'The Ship' Richard Church
4   'Outwards' (Anon)
5   'The Floating Ship' John Close – 10-year-old boy from a local school
6   'A Wet Sheet and a Flowing Sea' Allan Cunningham
7   'A Sailor's Thoughts' Laury Wain – 11-year-old boy from a local school
8   'Sailor's Delight' C. Fox Smith
9   'The Main Deep' James Stephens
10 'China Clipper' (unknown)
11 'Christmas at Sea' R. L. Stevenson
12 'Cargoes' John Masefield
13 'A Channel Rhyme' C. Fox Smith
14 'The Ship' J. C. Squire
15 Conversation between Captain Cat and Rosie Probert from *Under Milk Wood* Dylan Thomas
16 'The Cutty Sark' George Barker

'Tam O'Shanter' by Robert Burns describes the legend which gave birth to the name *Cutty Sark*. (Any programme of sea poems can be greatly enhanced by the use of suitable sound effects taken from BBC Sound Effects Record No 3 – RED 102M.)

3 *Sea shanties and seasongs*

Once again a large choice is available; most school songbooks contain a selection. There are a number of records which would enable the children to join in either the whole of the songs or just the choruses.

Farewell Nancy: Sea Songs and Shanties Topic 12T 110
Folk Songs of Britain (Vol. 6: Sailormen and Servingmaids) Topic 12T 194
Seasongs and Shanties Topic Sampler No 7
The Valiant Sailor Topic 12TS 232

A useful book for the teacher is:
Hugill, S. (1977) *Sea Shanties*

4 *Music/movement/drama*

Music of a different kind can be included in such a project for use in drama and movement work, or for listening to.

En Bateau Debussy
Allegro *Water Music* Handel
'Adagio' from *Spartacus* Khatchaturian (*Onedin Line* theme music)
Calm Sea and *A Prosperous Voyage* Mendelssohn
Fingal's Cave (Overture – Hebrides Suite) Mendelssohn
Blue Peter Mike Oldfield
Portsmouth Mike Oldfield
Overture from *The Wreckers* Ethel Smyth

5 Creative writing

Stories of the sea abound: Joseph Conrad's *Typhoon* and Eric Newby's *The Last Great Grain Race* (Pan Books) are two examples which will feed the imagination and stimulate personal writing from the children. Joseph Conrad was the first mate on a clipper ship; Herman Melville of *Moby Dick* fame was also a sailor on this kind of ship. *Bird of Dawning* by John Masefield is another novel about the tea trade and some of the exciting races which took place between clippers trying to reach Britain first.

6 Art and craft

Various traditional crafts can be introduced to older children, ranging from putting ships in bottles to knotting and splicing. Steven Bank's book *The Handicrafts of the Sailor* (David & Charles) provides illustrations and instructions on how to carry out the various operations. The making and sailing of model boats requires a high degree of skill, but interested pupils and their teacher could produce some seaworthy craft. *Model Boat Building* by Herb Lozen in the *Sterling* series provides some helpful ideas.

Other ideas

Tea Clipper Race by Rex Walford (Longman) is an excellent and relevant example of a geographical game which involves children in decision making, and provides insights into the effects of the weather on the success of a voyage.

Modelling the Cutty Sark by Edward Bowness (Model and Allied Publications Ltd) not only provides another account of the ship, but also gives detailed instructions on how to build a reproduction of it. It may be that the teacher will settle for something between the *Airfix* kit mentioned above and the Bowness instructions, but both art and craft can feature fully in this project.

The China Run from the Brooke Bond, Oxo Education Service (Leon House, High Street, Croydon) is an example of the kind of commercial aid which adds to the available resources for both the children and the teacher.

The Ship and Her Environment (Heinemann Educational for the Schools Council) is also aimed at secondary school students but a primary teacher with a bent towards science will find a variety of ideas which could be introduced to ten- or eleven-year-olds. Material available from the Education Officer, Beaulieu, Hampshire includes illustrated material on the work of the ship-builders of Buckler's Hard.

The Moon

The moon has fascinated both the scientist and the romantic for centuries. Children will enjoy finding out what people throughout time have discovered, believed or imagined about it.

> The moon is terraneous, is inhabited as our earth and contains animals of a large size and plants of a rarer beauty than our globe affords. The animals in their virtues and energy are fifteen degrees superior to ours, emit nothing excrementitious and the days are fifteen times longer.
> (Xenophanes, 500 BC)

> All the creatures of the Moon are either spherical or snakelike. Their bodies are covered with a thick protective layer, in plants consisting of a spongy, porous rind, in animals of a scaly armour, which in the course of the two-week day peel off in charred fragments. At evening apparently dead creatures like black pine-cones lie about, slowly reviving under the mild earthshine and becoming completely restored during the night.
> (Kepler, 1634)

> Once a warrior, very angry
> Seized his grandmother and threw her
> Up into the sky at midnight
> Right against the moon he threw her
> 'Tis her body that you see there.
> (H. W. Longfellow *Hiawatha*, 1855)

In 1865, Jules Verne was writing his stories 'From the earth to the moon' and 'Round the moon'. He was uncannily accurate in his predictions. Verne's projectile took 97 hours 20 minutes to reach the moon; Apollo 10 took 98 hours 10 minutes to cover the same distance; Verne's space craft was launched in Florida only 100 miles from Cape Kennedy. Verne also foresaw the possibility of a space race: 'As for the Yankees, they have no other ambition than to take possession of this new continent of the sky, and to plant upon the summit of its highest elevation the star-spangled banner of the United States.' Incidentally Projectile splashed down in the Pacific with a recovery ship in readiness.

These quotations and references are only a few of the different ideas which were held about the moon, and children can be invited to exercise their imaginations in a similar way. They can write about, draw and make models of imaginary moon plants and animals. The poet Ted Hughes has written a number of pieces on this theme (see *Poetry in the Making*, Faber), and the class might prepare sound effects to illustrate 'Moon Horrors' or 'Moon-Hops'.

Resources
Because of regular and thorough coverage by the media of the Russian and American space explorations, there are many resources, particularly in book form. Only a selection is given here.

Reference books
Ardley, N. (1978) *Man and Space* Macdonald Educational
Beckland, J. *Man on the Moon* ('Exploring Books' – Science Museum) HMSO
Branley, F. M. (1962) *The Moon Seems to Change* Black
Branley, F. M. (1964) *Rockets and Satellites* Black
Branley, F. M. (1964) *What the Moon is Like* Black
Gatland, K. (1976) *Manned Spacecraft* Blandford Press
Gatland, K. (1972) *Robot Explorers* Blandford Press
Kerrod, R. (1979) *Space* Hamlyn
Monday, D. *Rockets and Missiles* Hamlyn
Newsome, J. *Rockets and Satellites* Hulton Educational Press
Times Atlas of the Moon Times Newspapers

Fiction
Lofting, H. *Dr Doolittle in the Moon* Cape
Marshall, S. *Full Moon* Cambridge University Press
Marshall, S. *The Long Dark of the Moon* Cambridge University Press
Wells, H. G. *The First Men in the Moon* Fontana

Poems
Auden, W. H. 'Moon Landing'
Clark, Leonard 'Night Sky'
Davies, W. H. 'The Moon'
de la Mare, Walter 'Full Moon'
Dickinson, Emily 'The Moon'
Farjeon, Eleanor 'The Moon'
Kirkup, James 'Tea in a Space Ship'
Nimmo, James 'Space Travellers'

Nixon, P. 'Moon Fantasy'
Reeves, James 'Wandering Moon'
Stevenson, R. L. 'The Moon'

Music

Beethoven *Moonlight Sonata*
Debussy *Claire de Lune*
Holst *The Planets Suite*
Strauss *Thus Spake Zarathustra* (theme from *2001: A space Odyssey*)
Saint-Saëns *Phaeton*
Songs: 'Fly me to the moon'; 'I wish I were a spaceman'; 'Moonlight
    Serenade'; 'My rocket ship' *Singing Fun* (Harrap).

Charts

Earth Satellites Pictorial Charts Unit
Map of the Moon George Philip
The Moon Pictorial Charts Unit
Phases of the Moon Educational Productions
Space Probe Pictorial Charts Unit
Wall charts from Space Educational Aids Ltd, 27 South Lambeth Road,
    London SW8

Records

Apollo II – We Have Landed on the Moon EMI EST 326
Man on the Moon Phillips

Slides

Sets from Apollo Missions 9, 11, 12, 14 and 15, with texts from
Woodmansterne Ltd, Holywell Industrial Estate, Watford, Herts

Films

Eclipses of the Sun and Moon E.B. Films (1963)
Man in Space Disney (1958)
Rockets and How They Work E.B. Films (1960)
Space Exploration E.B. Films (1972)
Space Flight Round the Earth Gateway (1967)

Useful addresses

The British Interplanetary Society, 27 South Lambeth Road, London
    SW8 (leaflets, film lists, lecturers)
Central Film Library, Bromyard Avenue, London W3 (handles all the
    Apollo films)
National Audio Visual Aids Library, Gypsy Road, London SE2

Planetaria

The Planetarium, Marylebone Road, London W1
Greenwich Observatory and Planetarium
Marine and Technical College, South Shields; Tyne and Wear

Planetarium; Merseyside County Museum, William Brown Street, Liverpool

Planetarium, College Hill, Armagh, Northern Ireland

Other visits
Gallery 6, Science Museum, Exhibition Road, London SW1

Activities

1 *Moon flights*
Find out about rockets, control systems, communication, life-support systems, selection and training of crew, recovery of the astronauts and capsule. After a thorough study, a simulation of a flight could be prepared with role play inside the control HQ as well as in the module, a moon landing and disembarkation, scientific tests, sample collection, lift off for the second time and return to earth. Introduce hazards – the need to dock with another rocket – possibly a Russian space vehicle – etc. Sound effects can be created or borrowed, e.g. from *Star Trek, Dr Who* or some of the music suggested above. The BBC issue a record *Out of this World* (REC 225) which can be dubbed onto tape for use during a performance of the story.

2 *Craft work*
The children can make large- or small-scale rockets. If a small scale is adopted, then a space station can be built using waste materials; a moonscape could be created by another group using papier-mâché on a baseboard. Suitably mounted these two scenes could take their place in the drama described above.

Other space vehicles can be made to complete the scene. Perhaps a space city might also be built. Models of the universe can be developed using spheres of different sizes. These, along with assorted space rockets, satellites and space stations make good mobiles. If the walls are covered with art and written work, the ceiling may be all that is left to use!

Noah's Ark

In *Genesis* 5, 28 we are introduced to Noah. The following five chapters tell the story of God's anger and the flood. The story from the Bible can either be read or told, and discussed with the children. Most find the events as interesting as did the people in medieval times who watched the story being performed.

Artists of all kinds have been inspired by the story's symbolism. These poems, stories, music and pictures may well inspire the children in turn.

A different kind of planning matrix has been developed for this project. If time is available these and other options can be taken up (see Fig. 14, page 100).

Resources

Fiction

Ainsworth, R. *Noah's Ark* Hamlyn
Brook, J. *Noah's Ark* World's Work
Harris, R. *The Moon in the Cloud* Faber
Kendall, L. *Rainboat* Hamish Hamilton
Reed, G. *Out of the Ark* Longman Young Books
Stowell, G. and Gompertz, H. *Mr Noah's Houseboat* Scripture Union
Walker, K. and Boumphrey, G. *The Log of the Ark* Penguin

Poetry

Bell, J. 'Pluviose'
Church, Richard 'The Shower'
Davies, W. H. 'The Rainbow', 'Rain'
Fry, C. 'Rain on Dry Ground'
Longfellow, W. H. 'Rain in Summer'
MacNeice, Louis 'Glass Falling'
Stevenson, R. L. 'Rain'
Sassoon, Siegfried 'Noah'
Thompson, I. 'Rainy Nights'
Stubbs, J. Heath, 'The History of the Flood'
Muir, Edwin, 'Ballad of the Flood'
de la Mare, Walter 'Rain'
Wordsworth, William 'After the Storm'

Animal poems are available in prolific numbers. One collection I found useful is:

The Neighbours: Animal Anthology 'Fougasse' Universities Federation for Animal Welfare

Plays

André Obey wrote *Noah* (Heinemann), a play for adults, and there is a Chester Miracle play *The Deluge*, extracts from both of which the children will enjoy. Here is an extract from *The Deluge* with the spelling of the time:

> Camelles, asses, man maye fynde,
> Bucke and does, harte and hynde
> Beastes of all manner kinde
> Heare be, as thinketh me.

Films
Noah and His Ark is a film made by the Chandos School, Netherfield, Nottinghamshire. It is available on hire from the British Film Institute, 81 Dean Street, London W1. Not only is this an attractive and stimulating film to watch and use, it may also encourage others to make this kind of project record.

Video-recording of drama and other activities is now a reality in some secondary schools, polytechnics and colleges; it may be possible to persuade the departments concerned to come and film particular features of a primary-school project.

Music
Britten, Benjamin *Noye's Fludde* Decca/Argo ZK1

Britten, Benjamin *Peter Grimes* (storm sequence)

Flanders, Michael and Swann, Donald *The Bestiary of Animals* Parlophone PCS 3026

Horovitz, Joseph *Captain Noah and His Floating Zoo* (words by Michael Flanders) scored for 2 part voices and piano Novello Argo/Decca ZDA 149

Lord, David *The History of the Flood* (words by John Heath Stubbs) Oxford University Press

Saint-Saëns *Carnival of the Animals* CBS 72072

Sound effects: BBC Record Red 47N *Rain and Storm* (No 1); BBC Record Red 102M *Sea Effects* (No 3)

Activities

1 Art
Animals; animals entering and leaving the Ark; animals on board the boat. Felt appliqué pictures.

2 Craft
The Ark – building; sailing; animal masks and costumes.

3 Music
Sound effects from the story – building the Ark; the animals; the storm; the birds, landfall.

4 Movement and drama
The story of Noah, 'backed' by music created to provide atmosphere.

5 Writing
Aspects of the story – the captain's log; disbelieving accounts of those not on the voyage; the Noah family dialogue.

6 *Conservation*

There are constant reminders of the threats either to particular species of wild life, or to an area which is due to be flooded to make a new reservoir, or used as a new airport, etc. These live issues can be discussed with children to stimulate writing and improvised drama, or to give practical support in terms of money or protest where wild life is endangered.

Figure 14 Project 'Noah's Ark'

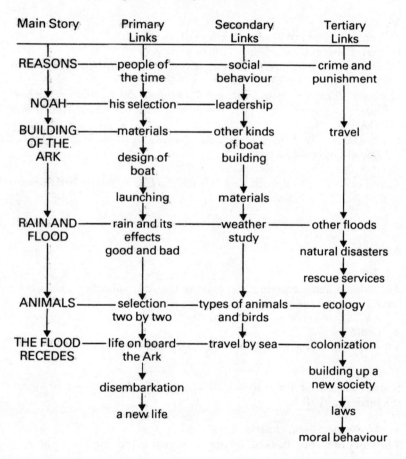

Vikings

In the year 793 portents were seen over the land of Northumbria and men were afraid. There were whirlwinds and phantom lights, fire-dragons flew through the air. Soon after came a dire famine, and shortly after that on 8 June of the same year, merciless heathens laid waste the Church of God in Lindisfarne with plundering and killing.

The Anglo-Saxon Chronicle

Thus the Vikings were seen by monks who found themselves under attack on a rocky islet just off the north-east coast of Britain. The Exhibition mounted in 1980 by the British Museum was at pains to put the record straight and present a picture of a race of people from Northern Europe as traders and colonists, as well as artists and craftsmen. Nevertheless, the Vikings lived in violent times, and as colonists and raiders they gave and expected no quarter.

Resources

Reference books

Cuardi, A. and Graham, J. *Viking Raiders* Usborne Publishing
Gibson, M. *The Vikings* Macdonald Educational
Henry, B. *Vikings and Norsemen* John Baker
Nichol, J. *The Vikings* Basil Blackwell
Peterson, P. *Vikings* Black
Platt, J. *The Vikings* Macmillan Educational
Wilson, D. M. *The Vikings and their Origins* Wayland
Wood, S. *The Vikings* Oliver and Boyd

Fiction
(to be read to the class)
Green, R. L. *Myths of the Norsemen* Puffin
Treece, H. *The Horned Helmet* Macmillan Educational
Treece, H. *The Last of the Vikings* Longman
Treece, H. *The Road to Miklagard* Penguin
Treece, H. *Swords from the North* Penguin
Treece, H. *Viking's Dawn* Heinemann Educational and Penguin
Treece, H. *Viking's Sunset* Penguin

Myths and legends
Asbjornsen, P. and Moe, J. *Popular Tales from the Norse* Bodley Head
Green, Roger Lancelyn *Myths of the Norsemen* Penguin

Figure 15   Project 'Vikings'

Aspects of the project	Possible activities

The people ⟶ Research

Family life ⟶ Writing/illustration

Social life ⟶ Drama and discussion

Origins ⟶ Map work

Expansion ⟶

Ships ⟶ Gokstad ship — models
Oseberg ship

Clothing ⟶ Sketch

Armour ⟶ Model

Myths and legends ⟶ Story-telling – improvised drama

Invasion of ⟶ Reference books
British Isles

Settlements ⟶ Paintings/3-D models

Place names ⟶ Mapwork/dictionary of place names

Culture ⟶ Religions, jewellery, costume

The Saxons ⟶ Story and reference books

King Alfred ⟶ Personal writing – after discussion and story

Modern-day Scandinavia ⟶ Reference books, holiday brochure Local people who have visited Norway, Sweden or Denmark

Kits
A collection of documents *The Vikings* (ed. Nickels) Jackdaw
 Publications
Middleton, G. *Saxons and Vikings* (Focus on History series) Longman

Charts
A Viking Settlement Pictorial Charts Educational Trust

Leaflets
Available from The Royal Norwegian Embassy, 25 Belgrave Square,
 London SW1

Films
The Vikings: Life and Conquests EFVA Film Library
Viking Ships Gateway Films

St Thomas à Becket

The martyr, Thomas à Becket is almost as well known as William the
Conqueror. His story is an interesting one; his rise to power through his
friendship with the king; his unwillingness to compromise what he saw
as his duty to his God, which surpassed his allegiance to his monarch;
his death at the hands of the knights who had heard Henry cry out,
'Will no one rid me of this turbulent priest?'; his canonization only three
years afterwards, and with it the displacement of other saints –
Edward, Swithin and Cuthbert – as the focal point for pilgrimage.

The project must be set in context and so the work of a monastery,
the medieval era, Chaucer can all be developed. Different aspects can
be covered by groups of children, who then present their findings
to the whole class.

Resources

Stories and plays
Anouilh, J. *Becket* Eyre Methuen
Eliot, T. S. *Murder in the Cathedral* Faber
Mills, D. *Thomas à Becket* Friends of Canterbury Cathedral
Mydans, S. *Thomas* Collins
Tennyson, A. *Becket* (in Complete Works) Oxford University Press

Poem
Dickinson, Patrick 'The Quarrel'

Kits
The Murder of Thomas Becket: A Collection of Contemporary Documents (ed. Loxton) Jackdaw Publications
Newspaper – devised by Frank Hooper School, Canterbury

Films
Becket Paramount Films
Murder in the Cathedral Connoisseur Films

Activities
Older juniors and middle-school pupils would be able to hear, read and see this story and discuss the various implications, in particular the conflict between Church and State, which was not simply confined to the latter part of the twelfth century. Although it would be quite demanding, the play itself could be performed.

When my own school worked on this project several linked activities took place. The story of Becket was performed as a play from within the project; it was later filmed (in 8mm) in the remains of a local abbey and in a very old church; children went to Canterbury by coach, in various costumes of their own choice and making, to represent pilgrims on their way to the shrine; a lunch stop was made on the Pilgrim's Way, with a walk along a stretch of the path (again recorded on film) and were picked up further along by a cooperative driver; the trip ended with a guided tour around the Cathedral whose organization of Friends had agreed to allow the children to remain in costume.

Some schools have walked the Pilgrim's Way from Winchester to Canterbury, staying overnight in youth hostels. The following publications (including of course the relevant OS maps) would be useful for teachers contemplating walking at least some of the Way:

Jennett, S. *The Pilgrim's Way: From Winchester to Canterbury* Cassell
Wright, C. J. *A Guide to the Pilgrim's Way and North Downs Way* Constable

My own favourite walking stretches are:

South of Guildford, St Martha's Hill to the Silent Pool.
Hollingbourne to Harrietsham.
A short section to the north of Lenham.
Two miles west of Charing to Westwell.
Harpledown into Canterbury (along metalled road – so sackcloth and bare feet may not be thought to be appropriate).

A study of the natural life of the chalk downs and adjoining areas can be carried on during such walks, and later written up and illustrated in the classroom.

Reference books
Lousley, J. F. *Wild Flowers of Chalk and Limestone* Collins
Sankey, J. *Chalkland Ecology* Heinemann

Chaucer
The journey to Canterbury, experienced at first or second hand, will include reference to Chaucer's *Canterbury Tales*. Not all will be considered suitable for eleven-year-olds, but some are. As well as hearing and discussing these, the children can be invited to tell their own stories. In contrast they might try to write and then tell their version of commuter tales for today.

This part of the project opens up a consideration of the whole medieval scene, with many opportunities for activities.

Resources

Reference books
Bailey, V. and Wise, E. *Medieval Life* Longman
Davies, P. *Town Life in the Middle Ages* Wayland
Hussey, M. *Chaucer's World* Cambridge University Press
Kendall, A. *Medieval Pilgrims* Wayland
Reeves, M. *The Medieval Village* and *The Medieval Town* Longman
Sayers, J. *Life in a Medieval Monastery* Longman
Unstead, R. J. *Kings, Barons and Serfs* Macdonald Educational
Unstead, R. J. *Living in a Medieval City* Black
Unstead, R. J. *Monasteries* Black

Fiction
Coghill, N. *Canterbury Tales* Penguin
Power, R. *Redcap Runs Away* Cape
Roberts, M. *The Fury of the Vikings* Chambers
Scarfe, N. *A Monk Called Jocelin* Chambers

Charts
Medieval Monastery Pictorial Charts Educational Trust

Filmstrips
Becket and His Times Educational Associates (212 Whitchurch Road, Cardiff)
Farmers and Craftsmen Common Ground
Medieval Britain Visual Publications
The Medieval World (Parts 1, 2 and 3) Common Ground

Films
Cathedral City GBI
From Every Shire's Ende Viewtech Audio Visual Media (Chipping Sodbury, Bristol)

The Medieval Monastery Rank
The Medieval Village Rank
The Road to Canterbury Rank

Records

Chaucer's Canterbury Pilgrims (disc and filmstrip) Educational Audio-visual Ltd (Mary Glasgow Publications Ltd), Brookhampton Lane, Kineton, Warwick CV35 0JB
Murder in the Cathedral Caedmon TRS 330
The Nun's Priest's Tale Argo PLP 1002
The Pardoner's Tale Caedmon 4FP 9007
The Prologue Argo PLP 1001
The Time, Life and Works of Geoffrey Chaucer (disc, filmstrip, booklet) Educational Audio-visual Ltd (Mary Glasgow Publications Ltd), Brookhampton Lane, Kineton, Warwick CV35 0JB

Figure 16   **Project 'Thomas à Becket'**

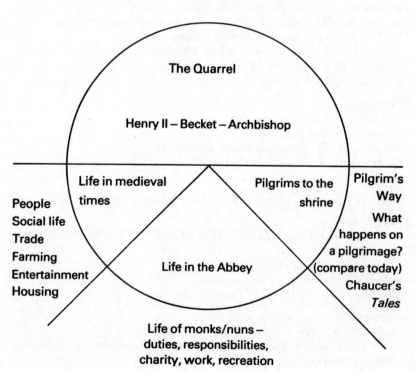

Activities

1 *Writing*

Accounts of the life of people of the times – the monk, the shopkeeper, the tradesman, the child, etc.

2 *Art*

Buildings of the period, costume, heraldry, armour, brasses, calligraphy and illuminated lettering, stained-glass windows.

3 *Craft ideas*

A medieval abbey, a diorama of a medieval village with simple cut-out figures of people and animals set against a series of low-relief buildings; a frieze of pilgrims on their way to Canterbury – the life-size cutouts of people and horses to be 'filled out' with papier mâché and then decorated.

4 *Drama/movement*

'Life in a medieval town', with sound effects, could tell the story of the arrival in town of some pilgrims with dialogue between them and the inhabitants – the innkeeper, the returning travellers, the blacksmith, the market tradesmen. Strolling players and music could complete the taped or live performance.

Kilcash

What shall we do for timber?
The last of the woods is down,
Kilcash and the house of its glory
And the bell of the house are gone;
The spot where her lady waited
That shamed all women for grace
When earls came sailing to greet her
And Mass was said in that place.

My cross and my affliction
Your gates are taken away,
Your avenue needs attention,
Goats in the garden stray;
Your courtyard's filled with water
And the great earls where are they?
The earls, the lady, the people
Beaten into the clay.

No sound of duck or of geese there
Hawk's cry or eagle's call,
Nor humming of the bees there
That brought honey and wax for all,
Nor the sweet gentle song of the birds there
When the sun has gone down to the West
Nor a cuckoo atop of the boughs there
Singing the world to rest.

There's a mist there tumbling from branches
Unstirred by night and by day,
And a darkness falling from heaven,
And our fortunes have ebbed away;
There's no holly nor hazel nor ash there
But pastures of rock and stone,
The crown of the forest is withered
And the last of its game is gone.

I beseech of Mary and Jesus
That the great come home again
With long dances danced in the garden
Fiddle music and mirth among men,
That Kilcash the home of our fathers
Be lifted on high again
And from that to the deluge of waters
In bounty and peace remain.

Frank O'Connor

This section will describe how 'Kilcash' was used as the starting point
for a project.

Frank O'Connor was an Irish writer and poet. I found myself drawn
to his poem 'Kilcash' whilst browsing through an anthology. There was
fortunately a recording of the poem read by the author (Frank
O'Connor Speaks – BBC REGL 2M).

Through an Irish student it was possible to make contact with a
teaching colleague in Eire, who provided background information on
the saga which had been written centuries before. Music written to
accompany the original poem was also sent to us. The headmistress of a
nearby school was an Irish nun. When I mentioned the title of the
poem to her, she recited it in the Gaelic – and then provided a free
translation!

The local school in Kilcash responded to an invitation to write. The
children provided a personal history of their village and the great
house, now in ruins. Pictures were included, as well as slides.

All this material was assembled in project preparation time, and when the children arrived they were greeted by an exhibition featuring a potted history of Ireland, provided by the headmistress mentioned above. The poem was read in Gaelic and in English, and then sung. Slides showing features of the ruined house were shown, and carefully matched to the relevant stanzas.

Various lines of enquiry were pursued by different groups. Firstly the children found more information and built up a context of knowledge. Then the creative work began with stories, poems and songs prepared by different individuals. Art and craft work included making large cut-out figures of people of the period. Two other features were food and drink, and entertainment. Efforts were made to create a simple and cheap Irish meal; we had a Ceilidh when we sang and recited to each other and danced to Irish pipe music.

'Kilcash' was also used as the basis for a weekend teachers' workshop. The following study programme evolved. It may help stimulate ideas about how the project could be further developed for children.

Study programme

Input
Background of Irish History.
Background to 'Kilcash'.
Reading of the poem (in Gaelic – in English translation).
Recording of Frank O'Connor reading the poem.

Process
Discussion. Use of slides. Examination of children's study of their village and their understanding of the situation.

Individual and small-group consideration of the following using reference material, and consulting with those with particular knowledge of the area, and its history:

1 Conquest of Ireland: colonization; landlordism; depression; emigration; decline.
2 Religion: St Patrick, the monks, Mass.
3 The Butler family: Lady Iveagh, Father John Lane.
4 Irish poetry and song: Gaelic; folk tales; humour.
5 Farming: forestry.
6 Birds: game birds, birds of prey.
7 Flowers: honey, mead.
8 The great house: building, landscaping, prosperity, dining, entertaining, decline, destruction.

Output

1   Writing and reading/speaking of stories and poems; songs, including choruses to involve everyone.
2   Pictures and models.
3   Feasting and dancing.
4   Insight into the fears, anger and unhappiness of a people.

Forty Starting Points for Projects

1   The study of a street; village; town; city – local survey.
2   Bridges: scientific and technological considerations, practical activities.
3   Weather: scientific observation and measurement; links with human, animal and plant activities.
4   Fish and Chips (and Salt to taste): three strands to follow – fishing, perhaps the most extensive; potato growing and harvesting; salt mining and panning.
5   The polar regions: conditions, exploration, animals, scientific experiment, tourism.
6   Journeys: to school, on holiday; voyages of discovery throughout the ages; mountain climbing; undersea travel; space travel.
7   Homes: different ages, different places; house construction – materials, services, decoration; animals and their homes.
8   Minerals: coal, iron, steel; manufacture.
9   Villains: pirates, highwaymen; forces of law.
10   The river: rain cycle; river geography and life cycle; man's use of rivers; crossings and settlements; plant and animal associations.
11   Animals: of British Isles, other regions; classification; life cycles; uses to man; conservation and protection – game parks, wild-life parks, zoos; individual animal studies; pets and their care.
12   The seasons: effect upon people, animals, plants; the annual change in trees; the work of the farmer; holidays; migration of birds and other animals; hibernation.
13   Health: the human body and its bodily functions; disease – prevention and cure; discoveries, e.g. penicillin, etc.; the work of doctors and nurses; a health service for everyone; dental care; exercise.
14   Seeing: the eye – colour, form, shape; optics – optical illusions; telescope, microscope; photography.
15   Festivals: Christmas, Easter, Harvest Festival, Pancake Day, Commonwealth Day; St George's Day, Hallowe'en, May Day.
16   Music: song – classical, pop, folk; instruments – making instruments, orchestras; composers; making music; music which tells a story – opera, ballet.

17 'Take a country': individual and group studies.
18 'Take a place of interest': Tower of London, Stonehenge, The Roman Wall, Trafalgar Square.
19 Regions and habitats: study the conditions of the area and the responses of people and plants and animals to it; deserts; mountains; hedgerows; underground; ponds, etc.
20 Famous events: Gunpowder Plot, Battle of Culloden, Fire of London, sailing of the Pilgrim Fathers, Norman Invasion.
21 Sport: national sports and pastimes; Olympics; training; inter-school competitions.
22 Entertainment and leisure: theatre, music hall, concerts, radio, TV; dancing; hobbies; spectator and participatory activities.
23 The saints: George, Catherine, Swithin, Francis, etc.
24 Mathematics: how people started to count; measurements; different aspects of mathematics; applications; problem solving.
25 Religions of the world.
26 Communications: methods of signalling; letter writing, the work of the Post Office; animal communication.
27 The North American Indian: history, culture, crafts, stories and legends; how the west was won – or lost; the Indian today.
28 The Football team: present-day position; the team – biographical details of players, trainer, manager; record this season – information about matches, results, position in league; ground, colours, details of former seasons; famous matches, successes; history of team and links with local industry, etc.; promotion/relegation; goal difference; distances to opponents' grounds.
29 Safety: in the home, street, school; at sea; in the air; underground; rescue services; accident prevention, training, need for rules, regulations.
30 A historical period: the Romans, Normans, Victorians – with the opportunity to experience through TV and film, radio and book what it was like to live in those times, plus visits to sites and museums where first-hand evidence can be examined.
31 King Arthur and his knights: read and dramatize stories; visit legendary sites.
32 Energy: human and animal – linked with food and rest; from wind, tides, rivers, sun; fossil fuels – coal, oil; nuclear energy; conservation measures.
33 Advertising: through the ages; use of billboards, handbills, newspaper and TV advertising; testing claims; comparing products through school consumer research.
34 Important occasions: Jubilee, coronation, royal marriage, royal tour, Olympic games, town or city celebration – good coverage on TV and in newspapers to provide background and make up for the lack of other resources.

35   How they built: our new school, new church, shopping centre, bridge; good cooperation possible through contractors.

36   Famous roads: A1, M1, the Dover Road, Ermine Street; include journeys along the particular routeway with stops at significant places.

37   Forestry: ancient forests; uses of timber; recreational uses of forests past and present; work of the Forestry Commission; linked industries – rubber, paper, rayon; animals of the forest – ecological patterns; life of the forester and woodman.

38   A wall: use of bricks and other materials; building a wall; purpose – weathering, gates and windows; plants and animal life; a geological walk – see *Stone in South Kensington,* a trail devised by the Geological Museum, South Kensington.

39   Write a town guide: better if this is a new enterprise or involves revising existing literature which is out of date or not written for children – library, town hall staff usually very helpful.

40   Money: swapping, bartering and exchange; place of money in the system – wages, prices, supply and demand; banks; stock exchange; taxes; practical applications.

Bibliography

Barker, E. J. (1974) *Geography and Younger Children* University of London Press

Cole, J. P. and Benyon, N. J. (1969) *New Ways in Geography* Blackwell

Cracknell, J. R. (1979) *Geography through Topics in Primary and Middle Schools* Geographical Association

Dept of Environment (1979) *Environmental Education in Urban Areas* HMSO

DES (1981) *Environmental Education: A Review* HMSO

DES (1972) *New Thinking in Geography* HMSO

DES (1979) *Sources of Information for Teachers – The Environment* HMSO

Douch, R. (1967) *Local History and the Teacher* Routledge

Haggitt, E. (1975) *Projects in the Primary School* Longman

ILEA (1980) *History in the Primary School* ILEA publishing service

ILEA (1980) *Social Studies in the Primary School* ILEA publishing service

ILEA (1981) *The Study of Places in the Primary School* ILEA publishing service

Lane, S. and Kemp, M. (1973) *An Approach to Topic Work in the Primary School* Blackie

Lines, C. J. and Bolwell, L. H. (1971) *Teaching Environmental Studies in Primary and Middle Schools* Ginn

Martin, G. and Turner, E. (1972) *Environmental Studies* Blond Educational

Martin, G. and Wheeler, K. (1975) *Insights into Environmental Studies* Oliver & Boyd

Mills, D. (ed.) (1981) *Geography Work in Primary and Middle Schools* Geographical Association

Pemberton, P. H. (1970) *Geography in Primary Schools* Geographical Association

Pluckrose, H. A. (1971) *Let's Use the Locality* (see series of associated *On Location* books) Mills and Boon

Scofham, S. (1980) *Using the School's Surroundings* Ward Lock Educational

Waters, D. (1975) *An Environmental Experience* ILEA

Williams, M. and Bell, S. (1972) *Using the Urban Environment* Heinemann Educational

Other useful books

Arkinstall, M. *Organizing School Journeys* Ward Lock Educational

Bassey, M. (1978) *Practical Classroom Organization in the Primary School* Ward Lock Educational

Beswick, N. (1975) *Organizing Resources* Heinemann Educational

Edwards, R. P. A. *Resources in Schools* Evans

Gordon, C. (1978) *Resource Organization in Primary Schools* CET

James, P. (1977) *Nonbook Media in Junior Schools* SLA

Jameson, K. (1973) *Junior School Art* Studio Vista

Jameson, K. (1968) *Pre-school and Infant Art* Studio Vista

Jarman, C. (1976) *Display and Presentation in Schools* Black

Leggatt, R. (1974) *Showing Off: Display Techniques for the Teacher* National Committee for Audio Visual Aids in Education

Lightwood, D. (1970) *Creative Drama for Primary Schools* Blackie

Marshall, S. (1974) *Creative Writing* Macmillan Educational

Morris, H. (1979) *Where's that Poem?* Basil Blackwell

Paynter, J. and Aston, P. *Sound and Silence: Classroom Projects in Creative Music* Cambridge University Press

Pluckrose, H. (1978) *A Source Book of Picture Making* Evans

Pluckrose, H. (1969) *The Art and Craft Book* Evans

Rosen, C. and H. (1973) *The Language of Primary School Children* Penguin

Rowntree, K. *Educational Technology in Curriculum Development* Harper & Row

Russell, J. (1975) *Creative Dance in the Primary School* Macdonald & Evans

Schools Council (1974) *The Educational Use of Living Organisms* Hodder and Stoughton

Schools Council (1972/3) *Environmental Studies Project* (Case Studies; Starting from Rocks; Starting from Maps; Use of Historical Resources; Teacher's Guide) Hart-Davis Educational

Schools Council (1975–9) *History, Geography and Social Studies Project 8–13* (Ceremonies; Going to School; Money; Packs; People and Progress; Rivers in Flood; Shops; The Victorians) Collins

Schools Council (1974) *Project Environment* (Education for the Environment; Learning from Trails; The School Outdoor Resource Area) Longman

Schools Council (1972) *Pterodactyls and Old Lace: Museums in Education* Methuen Educational and Evans Bros

Schools Council (1975) *Science 5–13: Using the Environment Nos 1–4* (see also Gaps and Cavities; Holes; Metals; Minibeasts; Ourselves; Structures and Forces; Time; Trees) Macdonald

Schools Council (1973) *Study of a Village* Hart-Davis Educational

Schools Council (1973) *Wiltshire Schools M4 Project – Birth of a Road* Hart-Davis Educational

Sutton, H. T. (1975) *Teaching with Models* Evans

Treasure Chest for Teachers (1981) Schoolmaster Publishing Company (Regular editions) available from Derbyshire House, Lower Street, Kettering, Northants.

Index